Milkyways

Milkyways

Camille Henrot

HATJE
CANTZ

Contents

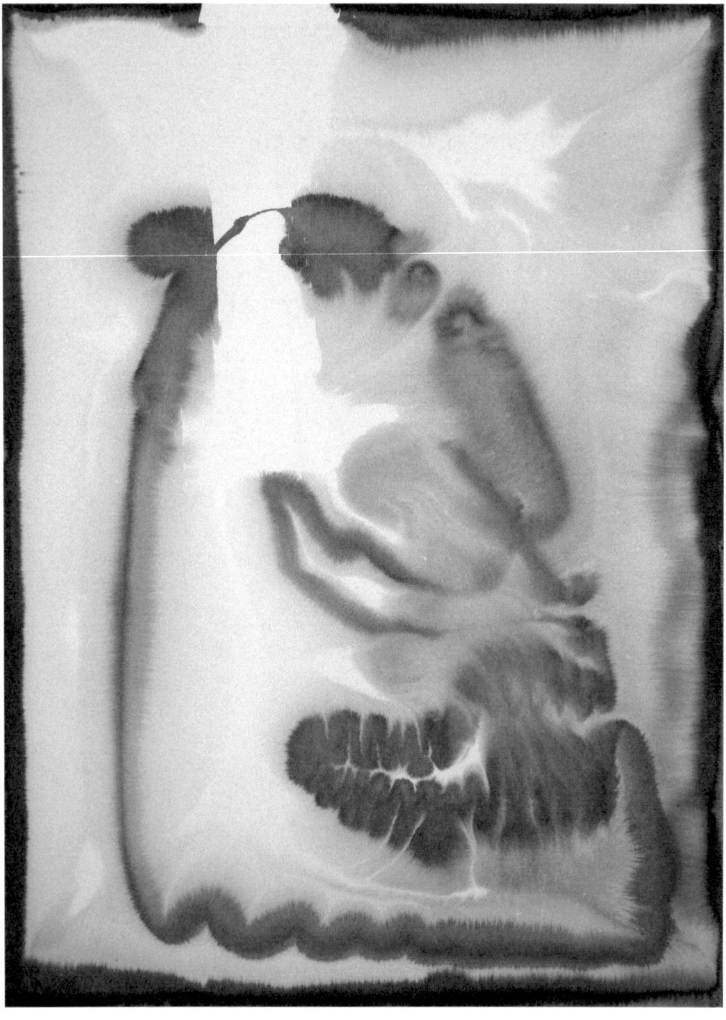

Untitled (Soon), 2019

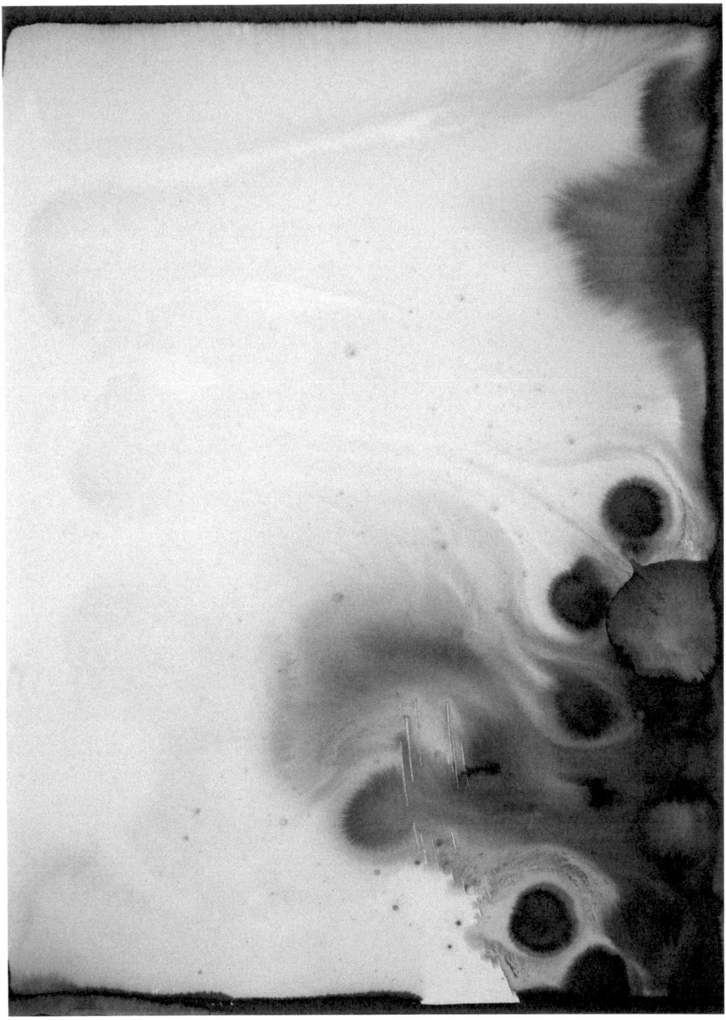

Untitled (Soon), 2019

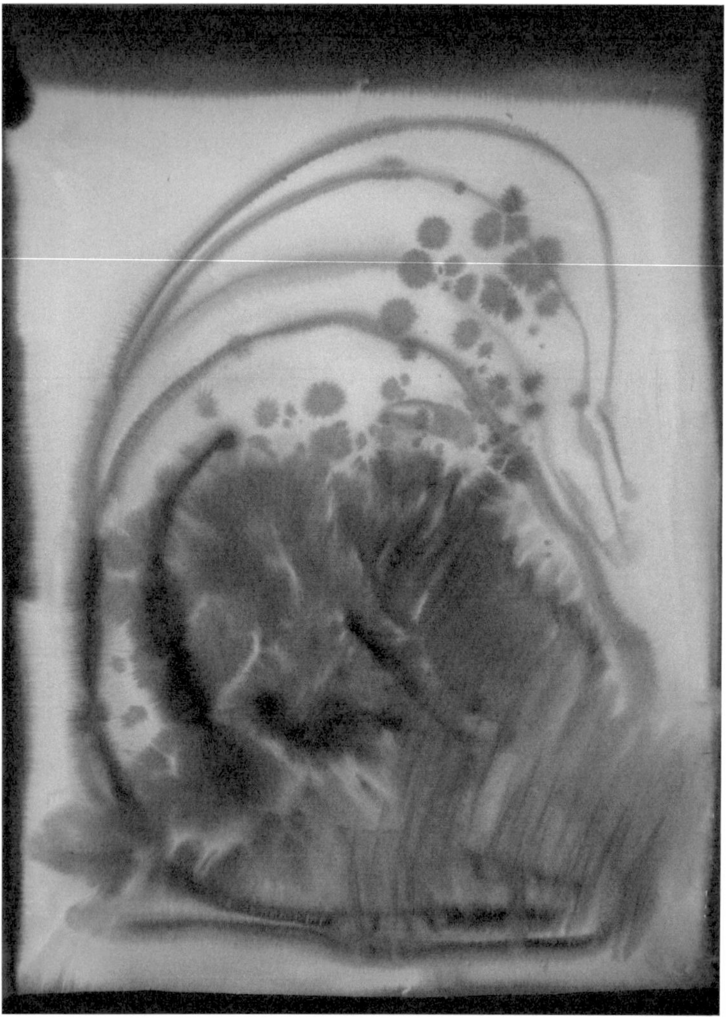

Untitled (Soon), 2019

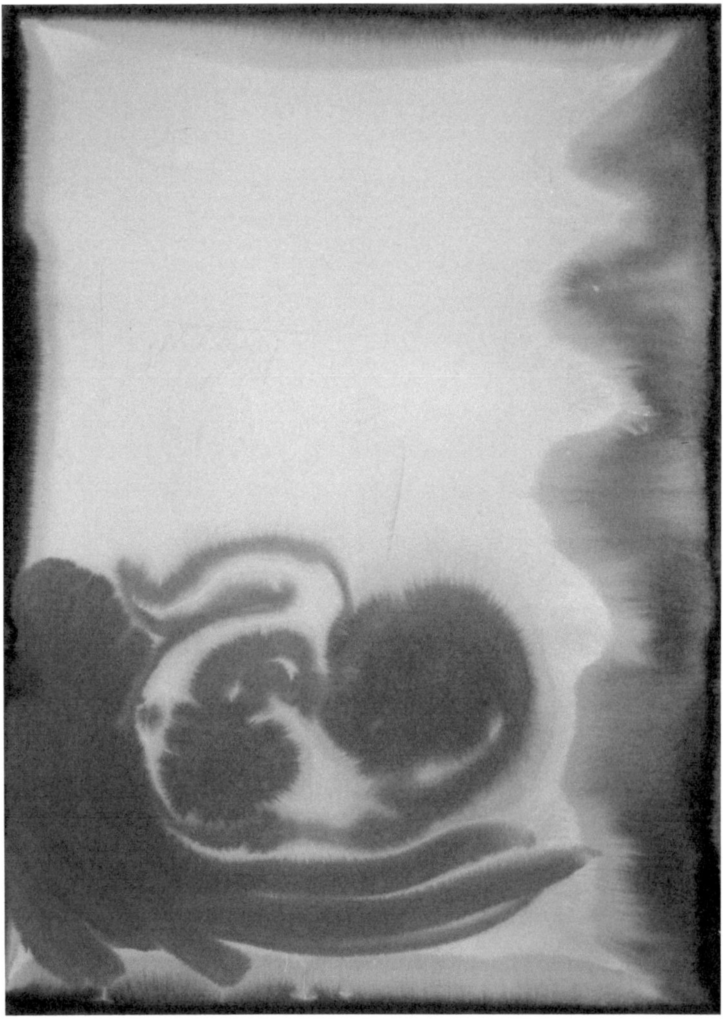

Untitled (Soon), 2019

Camille Henrot

Foreword

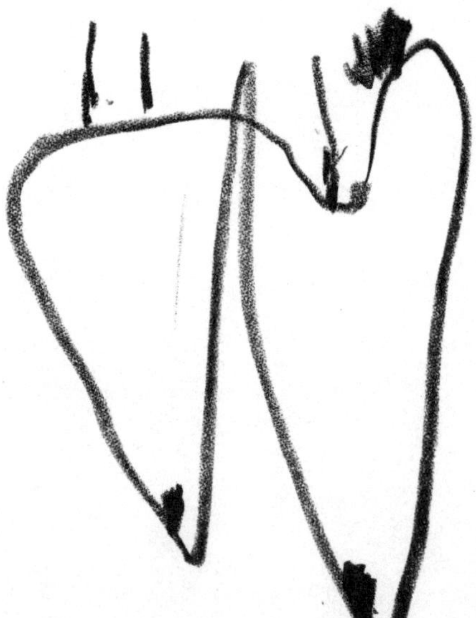

Drawing by the artist's son Iddu, 2022

Writing about procreation and motherhood feels like taking a brick out of a wall and watching the whole house collapse as a result. The image of Pandora's box comes to mind: on the outside, it's a precious thing, but once you open it, all the dynamics of prejudice, essentialism, relational dynamics, and power are exposed. The beginning of life is truly where all things start, good and bad.

Soaking in the intensity of my experience of motherhood, words became a vital resource. This book does not attempt to draw any sort of conclusion to these conundrums or resolve any conflict; rather it is a collection of sensations and thoughts, limited by my own experience in terms of culture, race, class, gender, age, etc. I also consider the limits of my ability to write in a language other than my mother tongue, as well as the way my mind works, leaning heavily towards monkey mind.[1]

Since I was a child, I've been perplexed by the idea of what it means to be normal. I wanted to change myself and the world around me so that I would be a "normal" child, and later a "normal" mother, but the more I thought about it, the more I accepted that this cannot exist. What we assume is common ground between us can also be the issues that are most divisive and impossible to resolve. There is no global image, there is no ideal mother, there is no good-enough mother: there are only many, many singular forms of care, or lack thereof. Although we are all "Of Woman Born," to quote Adrienne Rich, child care is still a topic that everyone has a strong opinion about.

The process of writing this book was messy and full of vulnerability, inconsistency, hesitation, and ambivalence, but ultimately I believe that these feelings are ones that I want to work with. It also feels unresolved in the sense that society moves fast. Statements that feel provocative now might feel banal in only a few years, if not sooner. In fact, it is my hope that this collection of essays may one day read like the key to a door that is already open.

I would like to thank Antje Stahl for initiating the column in *Republik* magazine, in which some of these essays appeared in earlier versions, and for her support in many moments of apprehension; to Jacob Bromberg, my longtime friend and collaborator; Léa Trudel, my studio manager and archivist; and editor Kimberly Bradley for making this particular dance-battle of the mind legible. Reading artists' voices on this topic has been vital for me in my own experience of childbearing and childrearing. I want to acknowledge most importantly the work of Moyra Davey in compiling *The Mother Reader*, and the inspiration of artists like Louise Bourgeois, Barbara Kruger, Alice Neel, and more recently, Talia Chetrit, Loie Hollowell, and Jenna Sutela. I would also like to acknowledge writers bell hooks, Ursula K. Le Guin, Maggie Nelson, Paul B. Preciado, Adrienne Rich, Jacqueline Rose, Suzanne Suleiman, Hélène Cixous, and my therapist Luis Alvarez. Thank you to Monilola Ilupeju for her thorough sensitivity read of several essays, to graphic designer Neil Holt, and to the publisher Hatje Cantz.

Thank you to my husband and the father of my children, Mauro, for not only taking on his own share of traditional mothering, but also for embracing and welcoming my sense of maternal ambivalence. I would like to thank my children Iddu and Sol for their pure sense of enthusiasm, joy, and lack of inhibition—a recipe for some of my favorite drawings of all time. Thank you to my mother Maud for being such an unconventional parent that the word "mother" never felt too narrow. Thank you to my older sister Mathilde, my second mother, and a well of unending support and intellectual energy.

Another motivation for writing this book is that opening discussions on these topics could serve to inform part of an alternative political approach to how we live and grow together. Mothers do not have to reinforce old systems; they can rather inspire new models of care, resistance, and innovation. My hope is that one day, motherhood will no longer refer to a fixed identity determined by gender, health, and reproductive and economic ability to care, but rather to a way of moving through the world. *Mother*, newly defined, is someone who stands by, stands close, and certainly, stands against.

1 Monkey mind or mind monkey, from the Chinese compound *xīnyuán* and the Sino-Japanese compound *shin'en* 心猿 [lit. "heart-/mind-monkey"], is a Buddhist term meaning "unsettled; restless; capricious; whimsical; fanciful; inconstant; confused; indecisive; uncontrollable," "Monkey Mind," *Wikipedia*, last modified on March 23, 2023, https://en.wikipedia.org/wiki/Monkey_mind (accessed April 14, 2023).

Antje Stahl

Introduction

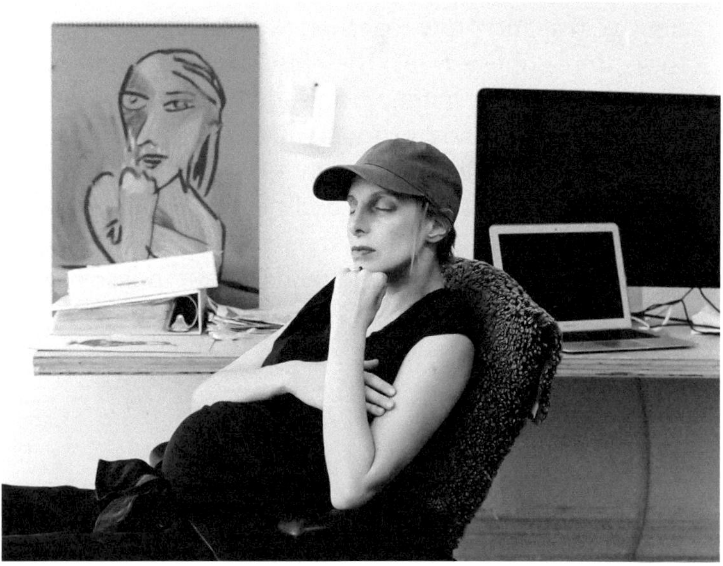

Portrait of Camille Henrot, 2018

Ever since I met Camille, she has been permeating her personal experiences with intellectual furor. So it was only a matter of time before she would transmute the *Milkyways* column into an essayistic volume and the artist book you are now holding in your hands.

In early spring 2021, I asked Camille if she might be interested in writing a column for the Swiss magazine *Republik*. It was the second year of the pandemic and we both lived in Berlin. Camille had started a residency at Callie's to facilitate the preparation of several exhibitions in Europe, including *Mother Tongue*, for which she assembled little dragons that cling to the breasts of bird creatures or facilely devour them in a flash. I suggested that we show a selection of these works on motherhood and contextualize them in short texts.

Ultimately I myself was trying to adjust to the torn life between breastfeeding and desk—my son was not yet a year old when I started working as a writer for *Republik*. And Camille's work felt like an aesthetic immersion of the experience that so many of us shared.

I vividly remember when I first saw Camille's sketches of a nude woman desperately trying to keep breast pumps latched to her nipples. It was in New York, in her studio on the Lower East Side, and her first son Iddu was still a baby. I thought I recognized the curator Jenny Schlenzka in these works, collectively titled *Wet Job*—I had worked for Jenny at the Museum of Modern Art long before she took over Performance Space New York as its first female director or even sat as a model for Camille. "Why isn't the genre of *Stillleben* (still life) transgressed by the subject of motherhood?" I asked, slightly enraged.

Stillen means breastfeeding in German, thus still life easily directs a native speaker's mind toward a breastfeeding life—and its transformative effects. We wearily sit still while the milk flows out of our bodies, alongside our awakened thoughts: in the presence of a newborn, our own existence is fleeting and all vanities vanish. Wouldn't everyone agree? A few years later, an online column by Camille seemed to be the right format to express these milky ideas.

So we started selecting images for the column, together with Léa Trudel, Camille's studio manager and archivist based in New York, and Nadja Angermann from *Republik*'s photo department. In addition to going through her series of paintings, drawings, and sculptures, Camille delved into her extensive material collection. She chose and shared underlined passages from novels and essays, notes for lectures, catalogue contributions, and exhibition texts that inspired a more essayistic approach than originally planned. We also met regularly in her studio (or at the playground with our sons) and had conversations that I recorded to catch the ephemeral aspects of mother-minds and our quotidian routines. And the more chapters we faced—each devoted to a different topic—the faster Camille's cosmos of thought seemed to expand.

It was summer by then, Camille was pregnant with her second child, and my father was dying.

Camille reached out to Jacob Bromberg for support. A poet and frequent collaborator of hers, Jacob entered the collective workflow on the essays, while caring for his three-year-old son in the southwest of France. *Milkyways* is thus the result of navigating both major life events and the pandemic parenthood balancing act, making for a complicity inside of this exceptional moment in our lives and in the world.

Some of these essays appeared in *Republik* between April and October 2021. Others were rewritten, and several new ones have been composed by Camille together with Jacob and Léa specifically for this book. Grasping the imagery and reading the essays, I again find myself in the *Milkyways* orbit. Here, everyday life with children has eliminated the boundaries between body and environment; everything is imbued with a longing for a transcorporeal existence and for conditions that nurture the needs of all of planet Earth's most vulnerable entities. Hopefully the result will be a flourishing of political thinking in the same spirit.

(Pro)Creation and its Myths

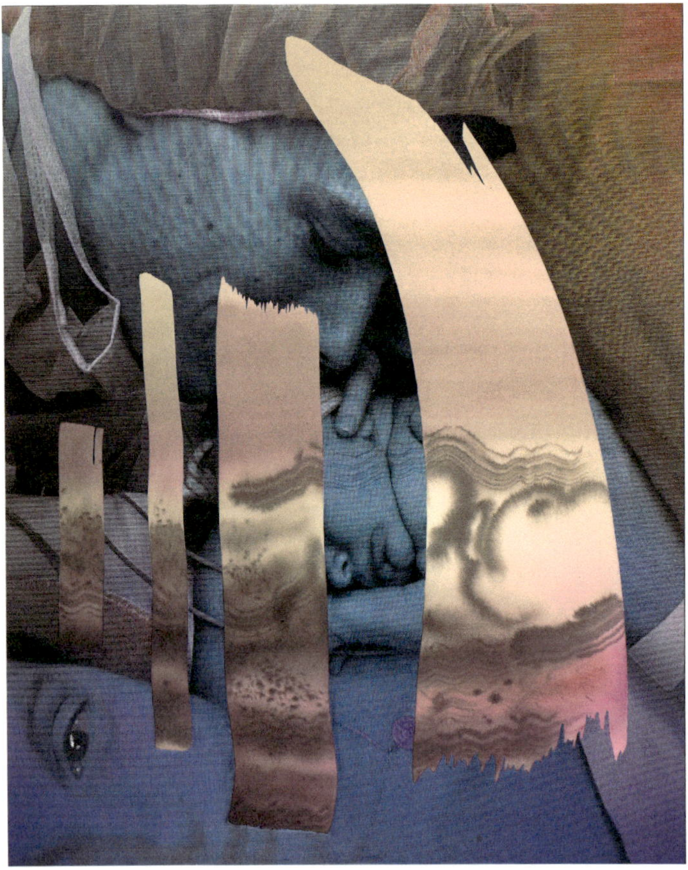

Dos and Don'ts – My Bio, 2021

Death and birth seem the most banal, inescapable, and yet defining moments of each human life. But while death has inspired countless narratives in literature, philosophy, cinema, and the visual arts, representations of birth have largely remained constrained to the realm of gods and myth. There is Venus, for example, who materialized naked and beautiful in a shell on the ocean's surface; Athena, who sprang from Zeus's splitting head(ache); Eve, who was formed from Adam's rib; and, of course, baby Jesus, via the Virgin Mary and the Holy Spirit. All of them came to life by way of male or divine fertility, detached from sexuality and pain, ignorant of the shadows of death—miscarriage, stillbirth, maternal death—and seemingly waterproof or otherwise unaffected by bodily fluids. It's enough to make one imagine that the emotional and physical reality of procreation and birth were simply not worth thinking about.

Creation and procreation are still mystified as quasi-divine manifestations located in the secrecy of studios, bedrooms, and hospitals. In Western culture, the two lonely archetypes of the Virgin Mary and the artistic "genius" exert a profound influence on the way we perceive the act of creation in artistic and domestic spheres. The work of the male genius was considered a god-given craft restricted to the chosen few by the church and the elite. Only the male genius was able to create masterpieces of such female figures as Venus, Mary, Athena, Kali, and Ishtar, obliterating women's experiences within the history of art. In this tradition, and in our paternalistic society more generally, creation has always been bound to self-sacrifice for women—either they devote themselves to a child or, if they are allowed, to their artistic vocation—but not both.

A few months after I gave birth to my second child, I decided to work on a series of paintings dedicated to this essential chapter in the lives of billions of women and men. I used a digital illustration application called Procreate, said to be designed for "creative professionals and aspiring artists alike," and which offers an extensive array of digital brushes that imitate the real gestures of painting. Interestingly, the moral and still very clerical patriarchal system that regulates procreation becomes muddled and uncertain of itself once technology enters the picture: in-vitro fertilization, egg freezing, sperm and egg banks, and artificial womb facilities demystify procreation in quite the same way that the digital tools used by so many artists nowadays demystify the creation of art.

I was born in 1978, the same birth year as Louise Brown, the first baby conceived by means of in-vitro fertilization. "As reproductive technology developed and entered mass culture, our theoretical inadequacies became glaringly obvious," Adria Schwartz writes in her essay "Taking the Nature Out of Mother."[1] Gender, heterosexuality, youth, and a healthy body no longer determine who can and cannot procreate, but money still influences who can raise their own children). Apple surely did not have this intention when it baptized its new app with a portmanteau for "professional creation" that seemingly demotes the work of amateur artists. Yet, the advertisement for the app suggests that it can replace a professional setup, allowing you to "work on the couch, on the train, at the beach, or while waiting in line for a coffee. It is a complete art studio you can take anywhere." While

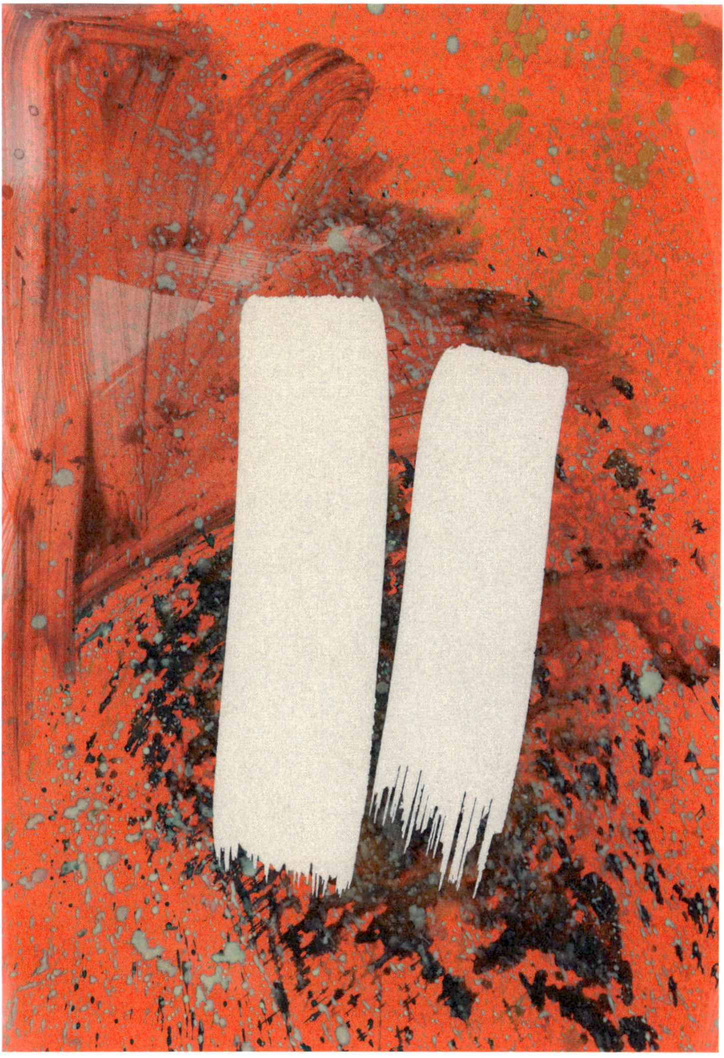

Milkyways, 2020

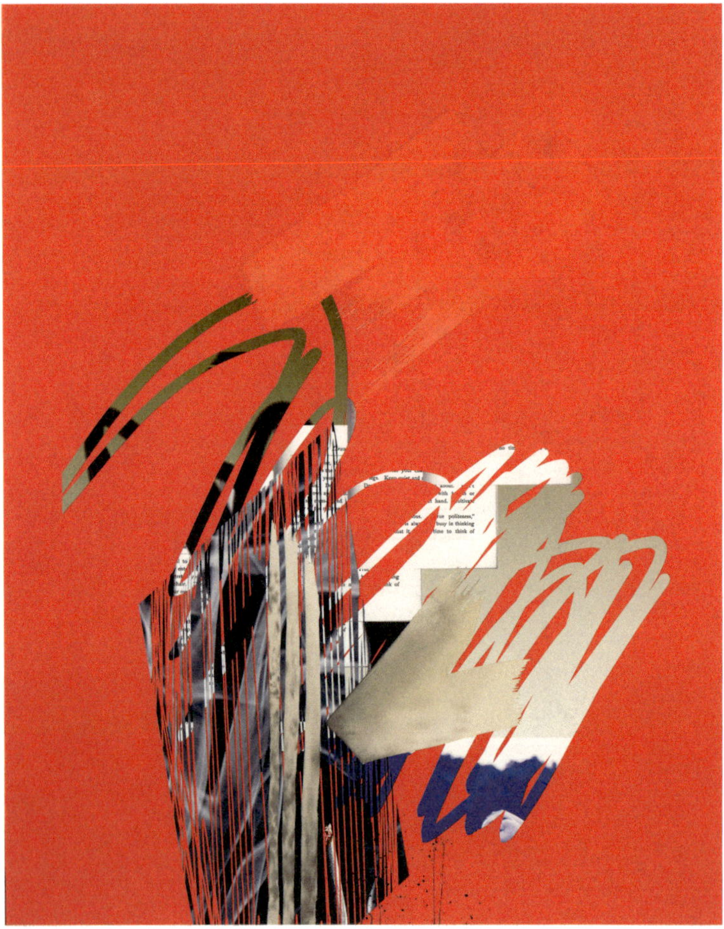

Dos and Don'ts – True Politeness, 2022

procreation "on the couch" might have been exercised as many times as there are stars in the sky, are we that far off from being able to digitally inseminate ourselves while waiting in line for coffee? What if in-vitro fertilization and abortion became as easy as a one-night stand? I wish my Photoshop virtual eraser could fade or crop out the fetishization of "natural" reproduction as instantly as it dusts out particles on a film's negative scans. With two fingers spreading and swiping on a graphic palette, we could in turn zoom out biological essentialism to expand to all forms of pro-creations.

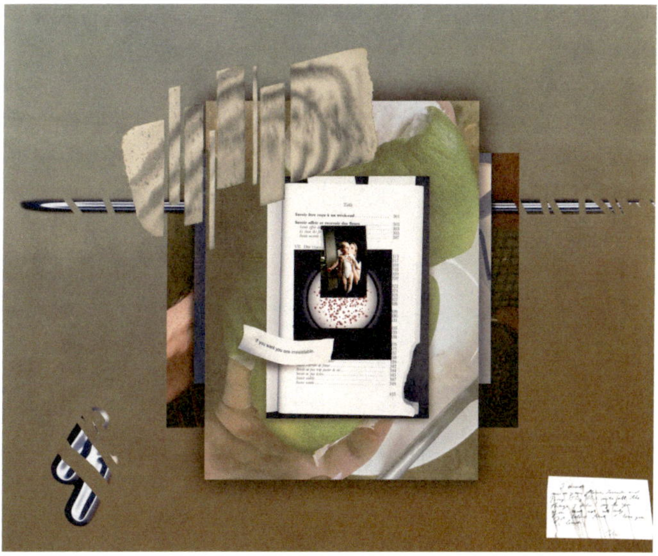

Dos and Don'ts – Just Believe, 2022

1 Adria Schwartz, "Taking the Nature Out of Mother," in *Representations of Motherhood* (New Haven, 1994), p. 240.

Rabenmutter or The Bird Mother

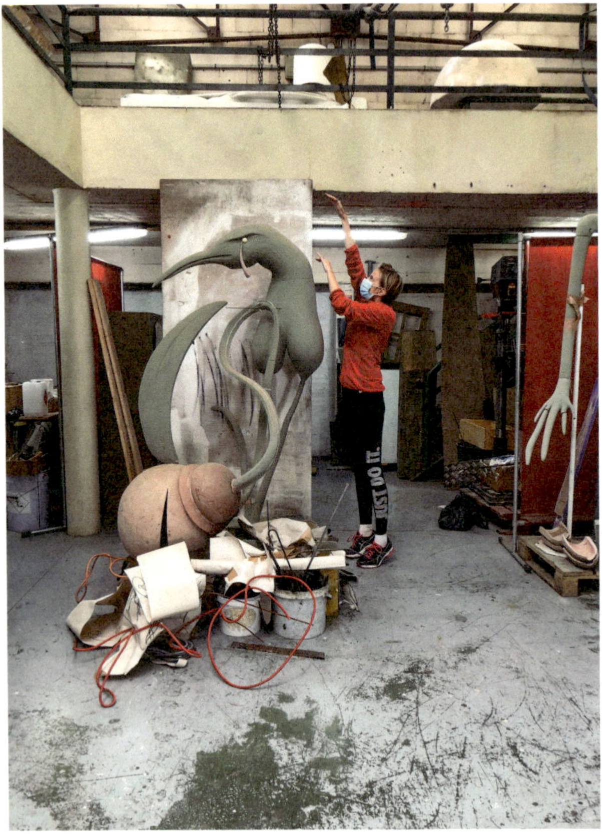

Making of *3, 2, 1...* (2021), Romainville, France

In the spring of 2021, I was working on installing my exhibition *Mother Tongue* at Kestner Gesellschaft in Hannover. It was the first time I was presenting a large body of work from my series *Wet Job* (2019), *System of Attachment* (2019–22), and *Soon* (2019–22)—a mix of paintings, drawings, and sculptures. The centerpiece of the exhibition, selected by curator Julika Bosch, was the largest sculpture I've made to date: *3, 2, 1...* (2021).

The sculpture was fabricated by the Swiss foundry Kunstgiesserei St. Gallen during the pandemic. Mauro, Iddu, and I had just left our home in New York City because my American visa was about to expire and government offices were closing as the city, like many other parts of the world, was forced into a strict lockdown. We landed in Zurich, where Mauro and his family looked after Iddu while I commuted to my residency in St. Gallen to work on the sculpture with the foundry.

I often felt guilty and ashamed for putting time and energy into things outside of domestic life—many "working moms" do. And the climate crisis has added yet another layer to this burden. The scientists Seth Wynes and Kimberly Nicholas published calculations indicating that global carbon emissions could be drastically reduced not only by eating less meat, taking fewer transatlantic flights, or living without a car—but also by having fewer children, or none at all.

Meehan Crist discusses these calculations in her article "Is it OK to have a child?"[1] She rightfully argues that the focus on individual responsibility for our carbon footprints needs to be shifted onto political and economic institutional actors. She points out that it was the fossil fuel industry that "carefully crafted and drilled" the "narrative that you, personally, are responsible for the climate crisis" in the first place. Since 2005, British Petroleum has apparently invested around 100 million dollars per year into a US media campaign promoting online calculators for individuals to work out their own carbon footprints, as well as toolkits for schoolchildren to kickstart their guilt from an early age. And—"fun" fact—Crist was invited to give a lecture in the British Museum's BP Lecture Theatre. But while such morally dubious sponsorships have increasingly been targeted by artists and activists in recent years, it hasn't kept us from getting bogged down in our guilt trips, to the point where the art world has also loudly raised the question: "Is it okay to make art?"

I won't say all the answers I've found have been satisfying. I'm guessing the whole knot will probably just continue tightening inside me as an unresolved, ambivalent feeling. Every work of art produces waste—scraps and shavings of materials that are discarded in the process of creation. While making *3, 2, 1...* in St. Gallen, I wanted to give shape to this ambivalence, so I collected and rearranged discarded materials at the base of the sculpture like the twigs, grass, and leaves of a nest. The crying bird at the center of the piece provides shelter for its young that paradoxically exposes them to the dangers of the world beyond.

Only recently, when we were living in Berlin, did I discover the term *Rabenmutter*. It literally means "raven mother," but the expression is meant to call out a bad mother who, like the raven, neglects her offspring and kicks them out of the nest "too early." I was surprised the term wouldn't instead associate

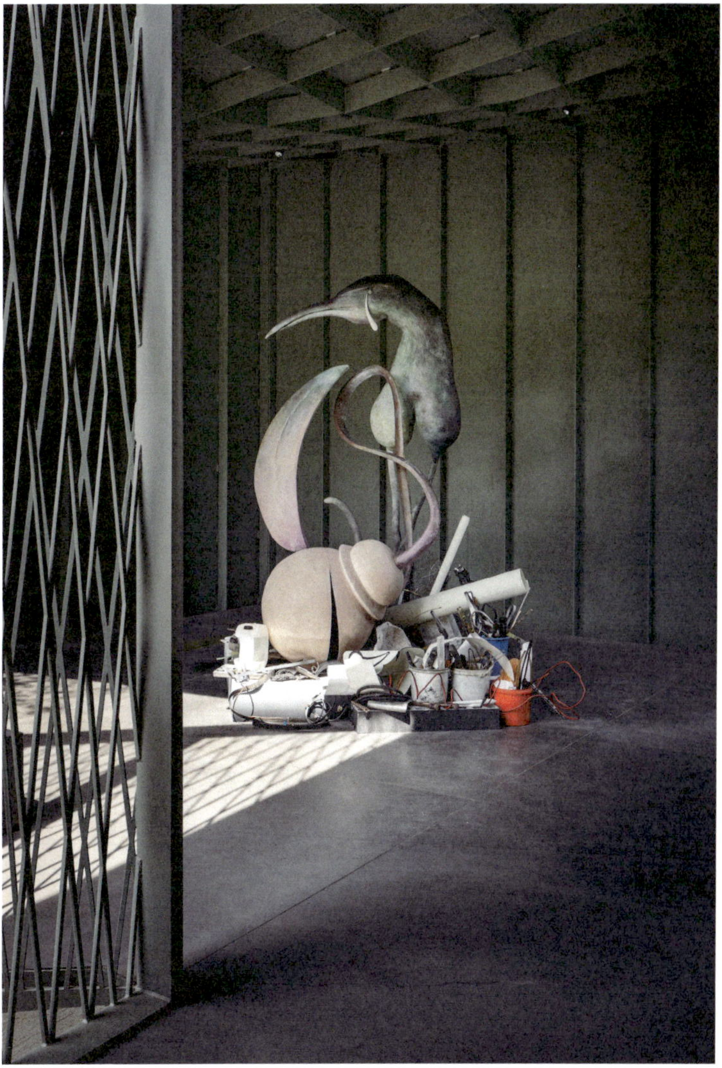

3, 2, 1…, 2021, Exhibition view, *Wet Job*, Middelheim Museum, 2022

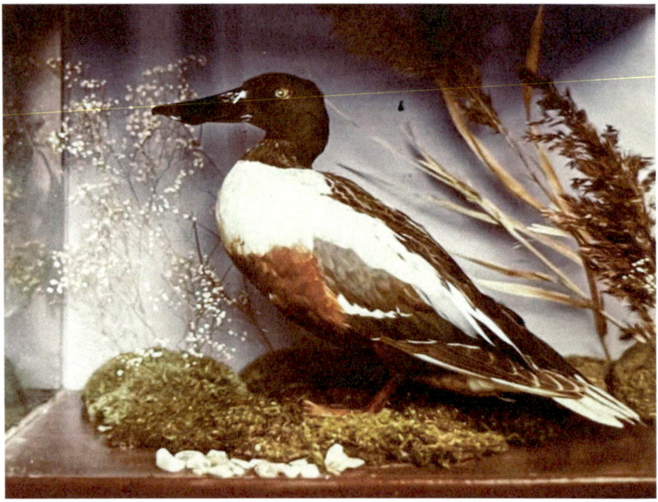

Henrot's mother's taxidermied bird displays, ca. 1988, Paris, France the mother with all of the strength that the bird represents in mythology, or with its scientifically-attested intelligence.

Growing up, I always loved how my mother could imitate bird sounds and songs. She worked as an artist and also as a bird taxidermist for the Natural History Museum of Paris, where she would prepare the animals for an eternal life. In our apartment, one room was filled with all sorts of metallic wires, stuffing materials, feathers, dried plants, and props. There was a drawer full of fake eyes of different colors. I wasn't allowed to play in there, and the one day I did, the eyes all fell out and went rolling all over the place.

I remember feeling deeply ambivalent toward my mother's work. Like all children, I was proud of what she could do, but I resented the activities that kept her away from me. A child's expectations are infinite and impossible to meet, and mothers will never be perfect, no matter how hard they try. But baby ravens, once strong enough, ultimately fly away, never to return. Childhood and motherhood are fleeting.

In this sixth extinction, our own nest, the Earth, has become an accumulation of our own waste. The visible evidence of the overwhelming detritus of humanity's (over)creation evokes the melancholy of an empty birds' nest.

1 Meehan Crist, "Is it OK to have a child?" *London Review of Books,* Vol. 42, No. 5 (March 5, 2020).

Echoverse

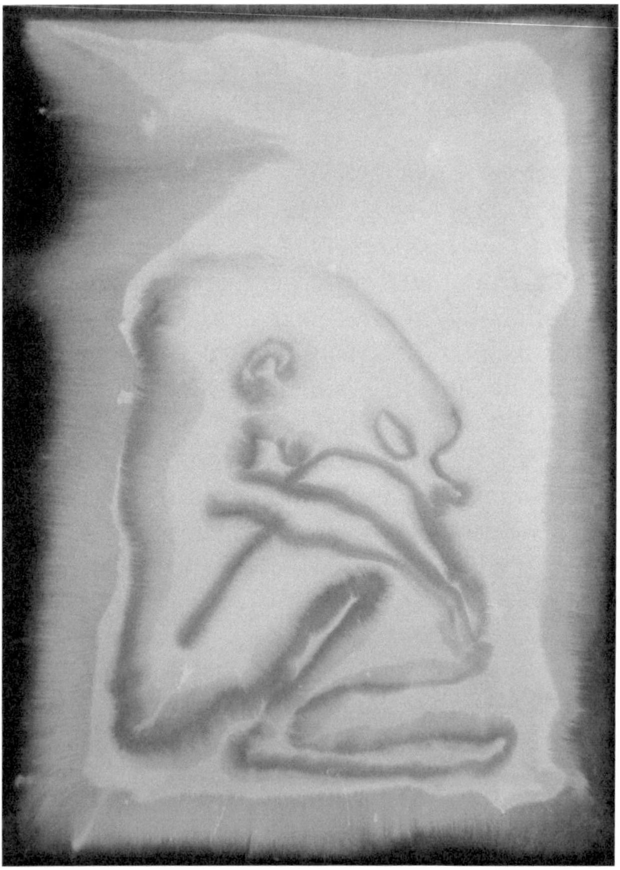

Untitled (Soon), 2019

When I was pregnant with my son Iddu, I experimented with ink drawings on heavyweight paper soaked with water. The diluted gradients and grayscale resembled photography, or more specifically, echography. Echography, or sonography, converts high-frequency sound waves, inaudible to our ears, into images of the soft tissues inside our bodies—the parts that otherwise would remain invisible. The drawings, inspired by my visits to my OB/GYN at the time, exist between abstraction and figuration—an absence or a presence of life. Some of the drawings show nothing but a blank watered space, whereas others house monstrous or deformed figures. I named the series *Soon*.

Echography helps to determine whether an egg has been fertilized and nested into the lining of the uterus. In other words, it can confirm whether there is a pregnancy or not. It can also detect whether the fetus shows abnormalities, is at risk for mental or physical disabilities, and even is at risk for premature death. The French psychiatrist Luis Alvarez, author of *Psychologies et psychiatrie de la grossesse* (*Psychology and Psychiatry of Pregnancy*), claims that these monitoring sessions are a very delicate and potentially dramatic stage in a pregnancy.[1] He described the woman at the doctor's office lying horizontally, vulnerable, half-naked, in a passive position, waiting to hear the doctor's assessment. Everything the doctor does—from their facial expressions to their tone of voice and choice of words—is subject to overinterpretation. "The doctor and the pregnant woman come from different universes," he writes—the doctor looks for a determination of health, and the pregnant woman is in search of meaning.

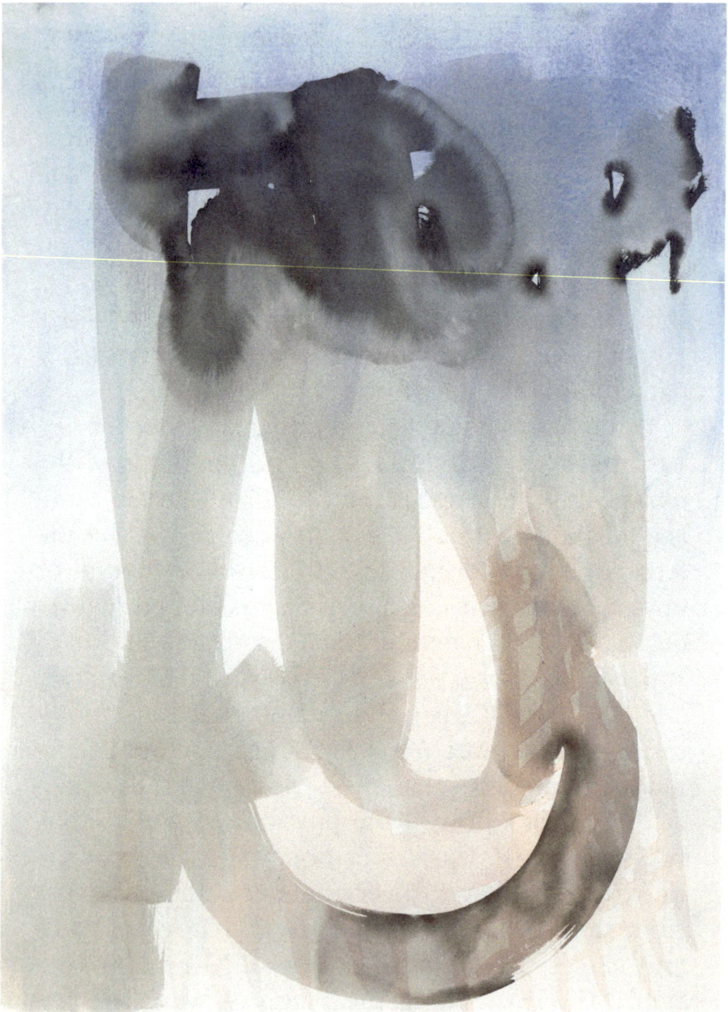

Untitled (Soon), 2019

In all of my pregnancies, I recall that the doctor identified complications on the screen; two of which were ruled out as viable. My visual reading of the sonogram was full of projection, like a Rorschach test. Alvarez speaks of a conflict between scientific image and *l'enfant imaginaire,* or "the imaginary child"—a child that takes on a life of its own in our heads, regardless of whether you have a child. The imaginary child is the dream child that we envision when we're little, when we understand that one day we will also become adults and have the capacity to reproduce and care for a child. This child is an idea that remains forever unborn.

While he was in the womb, Iddu often reacted to the echography as if he were trying to escape our view. I felt empathy for his desire to stay invisible, floating in the liquid darkness, unwilling to share the black-and-white or sepia-tinted surveillance footage that was made of him.

Echography inevitably recalls the myth of Echo, known best from Ovid's *Metamorphoses* but originating in Greek mythology. Echo was an Oread (a kind of mountain nymph) that Zeus tasked with distracting his wife Hera by talking to her incessantly, in order to keep her occupied while he amused himself with other women. When Hera found out about this, she took away Echo's ability to speak, allowing her only to repeat the last words spoken by another. Echo couldn't tell Narcissus that she was in love with him; but he rejected her anyway, like all the others who had fallen for him. Heartbroken, Echo retreated into a cave and refused to eat. After her death, her bones turned to stone, forever producing what we call an echo. In this story, love and communication constantly fail.

Echoes, imitation, and misunderstandings have also found their way into the work of my son's father, Mauro Hertig. In his piece "Mum Hum," he positions two pairs of musicians on each side of a long tin-can telephone. While the performers on one side play from the score, much like in a normal classical concert setup, those on the other side listen and imitate the sounds from the senders, creating a flow of echoes. Like in the children's game Telephone, the senders' melodies get distorted and falsified until nothing remains but a stream of mumbles and beeps. Taking inspiration from what an unborn child can hear inside the mother's womb, "Mum Hum" creates a stage environment in which one side of the telephone represents the outside world and the other side is the soundscape of the fetus—mumbled speech, numbed melodies. The mother's body, which both grows and protects the fetus, turns out to be a falsifier of outside sounds, filtering them through its layers of skin, fat, and liquid before it reaches the fetus's ears. What the unborn child receives is only ever an echo of the outside world.

Mauro Hertig's "Mum Hum" was recorded for WDR3 with Ensemble Garage and broadcast on April 23, 2021. It was later performed at Wittener Tage für Neue Kammermusik in April 2022.

1 Luis Alvarez and Véronique Cayol, *Psychologies et psychiatrie de la grossesse* (Paris, 2015).

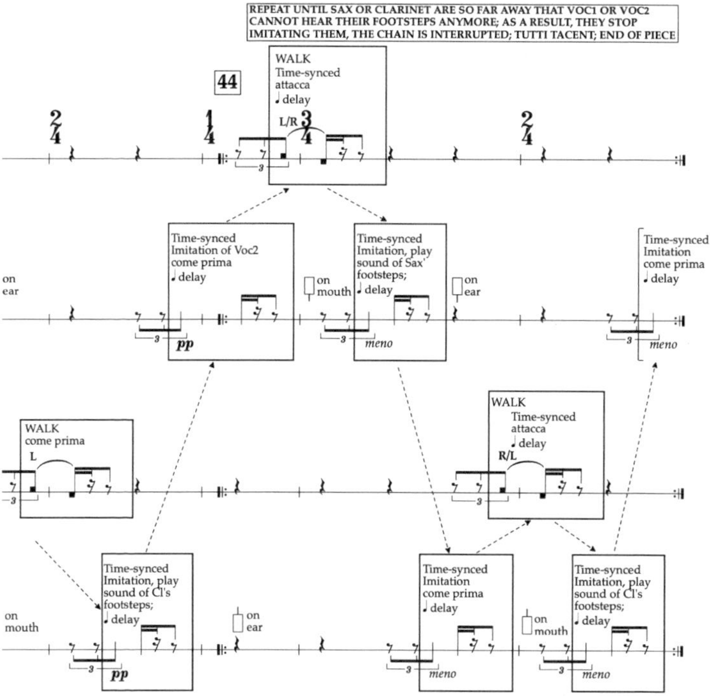

Excerpt from the score "Mum Hum" by Mauro Hertig, 2021

Please Do Not Touch

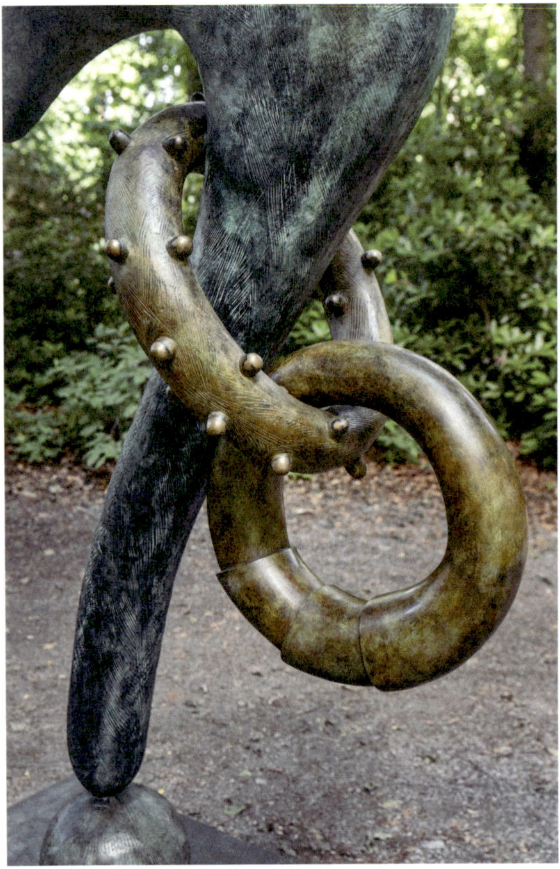

Every Goodbye (detail), 2019

Before they start to speak, babies try to put everything within reach into their mouths. They also love to reach out to their parents' mouths while being fed. When Iddu was little, I had the impression that by literally putting his fingers into my mouth, he was trying to catch the words coming out of the space between my lips. It was as if he were trying to find answers to the questions: "Where do words come from? How do these people manage to speak?"

In the absence of language, babies, like puppies, seek to understand objects by putting them into their mouths. Through the resulting sensations, a primeval form of "understanding" emerges. I started to imagine how the world might exist before words, and the way that words themselves are shaped. These thoughts became unresolved questions in my work, because reading gestures and projecting oneself into the child's preverbal world is crucial for caregivers, even if one inevitably bumbles through much of it. You have to somehow return to preverbal childhood in order to understand what the child needs, entering an intense present with virtually no past or future (and thus no patience).

Today, at four years old and capable of expressing his feelings with words, Iddu continues to grasp at objects as if to try to understand what their essence might be. One day, I was lying on the sofa with Mauro's head in my lap, my hands stroking his face. Mauro asked me whether I was caressing him or wanting to analyze his head's shape, as if I were going to make a sculptural model of it. I responded: "Both, I think." "Iddu does the same," Mauro said, "he caresses and explores at the same time."

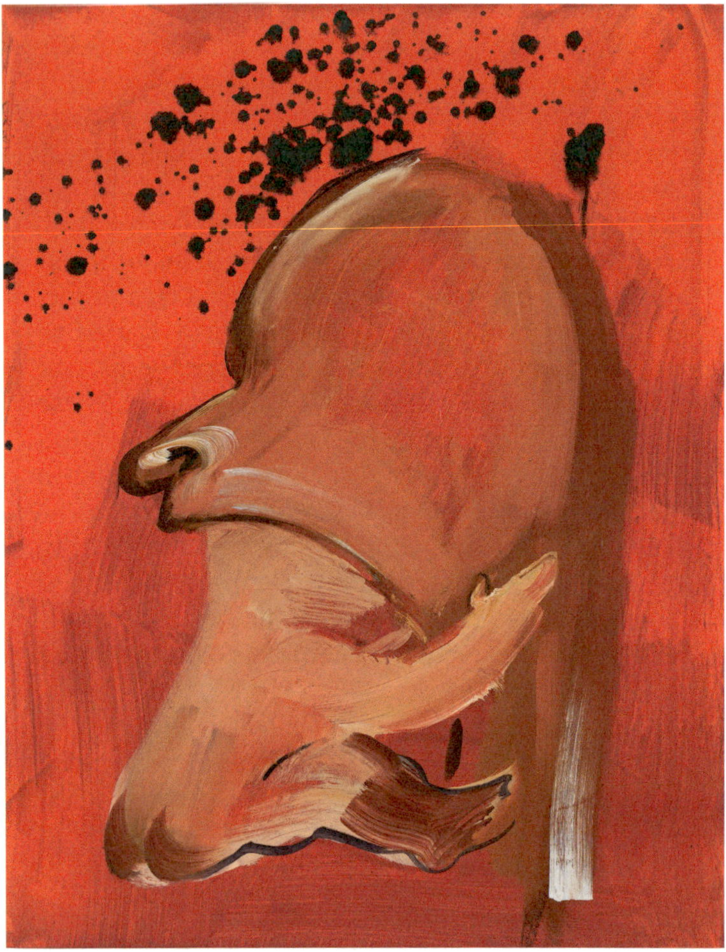

Words of Mouth, 2020

As an artist and especially as a sculptor, tactility is an enlightening concept for me. I like for all of my works to have a visceral, physical quality, even in film. A successful sculpture is one that, among other things, for me, triggers the urge to touch.

In a museum, one might encounter a sign warning "Please do not touch." No touching is a cardinal rule when visiting museum exhibitions, though it doesn't prevent people from approaching the artworks. We can learn a lot about human desire by analyzing the areas on sculptures where the patina has faded, or the stone is most polished. In the Botanical Gardens in Florida, I once saw a sculpture of a female figure made of stone, guarded by one of these signs. It showed the traces of many hands all concentrated on two spots: her breast and her belly. In *The Pleasure of the Text,* Roland Barthes writes, "The writer is someone who plays with his mother's body."[1] Is sculpture's subversive purpose to serve as a substitute for the

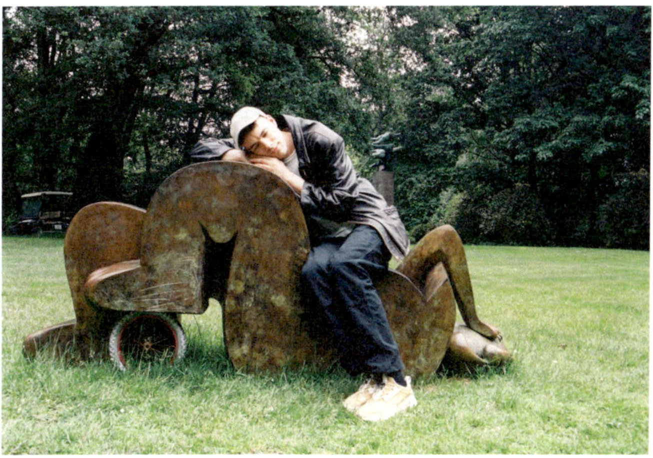

Mauro and *Derelitta*, 2016, at Middelheim Museum, 2022

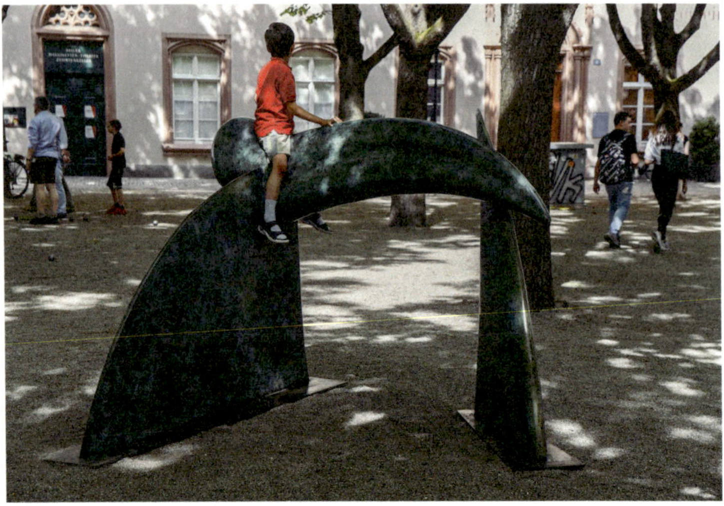

Inside Job, 2019, at Art Basel Parcours, 2019

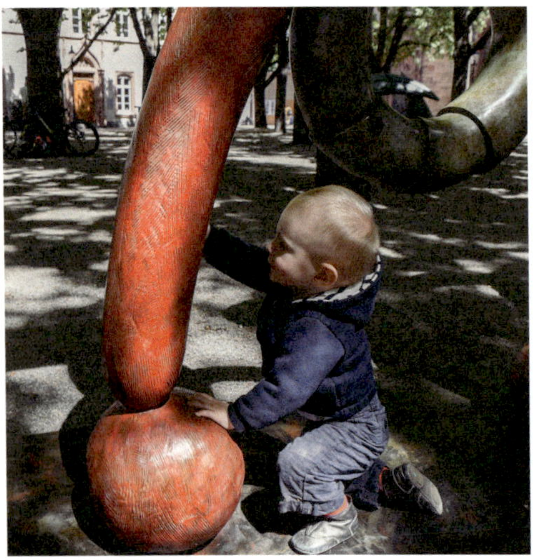

Iddu and *Every Goodbye*, 2019, at Art Basel Parcours, 2019

mother's body when they are no longer within reach? Do sculptures also stand in as substitutes for language, for intimacy, for our need to feel cared for?

In 2019, I showed several large-scale sculptures on Münsterplatz in downtown Basel at Art Basel Parcours, a public art event curated by Samuel Leuenberger. *Every Goodbye* is a larger-than-life series of question marks with a baby teether, referencing my meditation on the origin of words. This was before the pandemic hit, and many of the kids who saw the sculptures instinctively climbed onto them, riding them like horses. Seeing this made me feel like my work was complete.

Later, during the pandemic, the pleasure of touch was taken away from us by Covid-19 and the reactions it required and inspired. I don't think we've yet fully understood the impact this condition has had. The effects of touching and not touching, paradoxically, seem intangible.

1 Roland Barthes, *The Pleasure of the Text* (New York, 1975), p. 37.

Maison Absolue

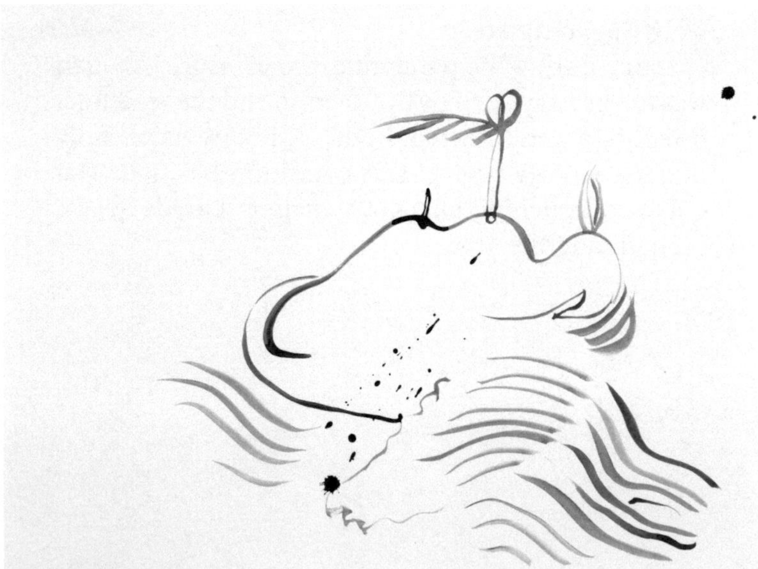

The Island / Mothership, 2018

My son's favorite illustrated children's book is called *La Tempête* (The Storm), by Florence Seyvos and Claude Ponti. It is about a little mouse named Clarisse and her mom and dad, who seek refuge under a huge blanket in her bed as a storm approaches. They bring their most cherished objects with them, as well as provisions—café au lait and ladyfinger biscuits—and a radio. The storm rages, destroying their home, and their tent-bed is the only thing left standing the next morning. This tent-bed is their mobile refuge—a protected space within which they can embark on exciting imaginary adventures.

At home, when we open the windows and air out the apartment, Iddu likes to hide under my bedsheets and imagine we are in our own little sanctuary, pretending to serve me coffee and chocolate. We call this game "La Tempête," and I really enjoy playing it, too. It embodies a fantasy that we can all relate to, like the feeling of getting to stay home from school on a snow day. The fantasy is one of total self-sufficiency and autonomy—a comforting, protected, safe space that is shared with loved ones and perfectly equipped with only the most essential treats you love and need. It is a space that incites a sense of escapist refuge, where you are released from the demands of responsibilities and an ideal form of intimacy can flourish. At the start of the Covid-19 crisis, when the first shelter-in-place order was enacted and before the impact of the pandemic was truly felt, I think many of us quietly relished the idea of not having to participate in a life beyond the confines of our home. Noah's Ark might be the origin of that home-refuge idea. As a boat, the Ark simultaneously offers both a place to live and the freedom of mobility, just like the tent-bed in *La Tempête*.

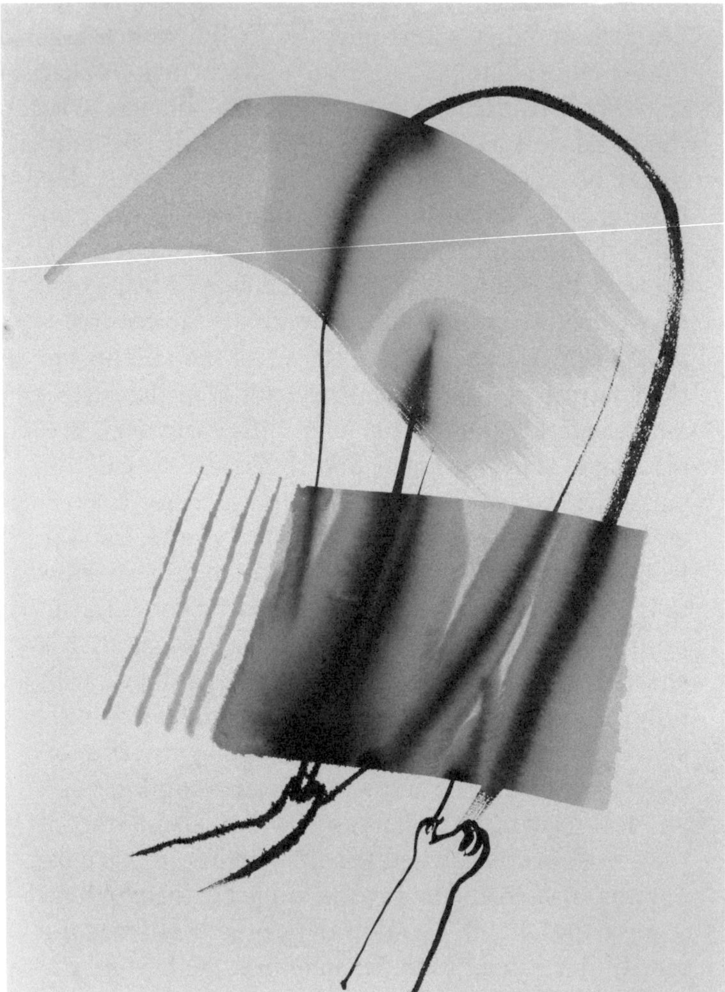

Gus Gus DA DA 1, 2019

In his lectures given at the College de France in 1977, entitled *Comment Vivre Ensemble* (How to Live Together), Roland Barthes defined this idea as the *maison absolue* (the total home).[1] This space is protected, hidden, and acts as a defense of an interiority that allows us to imagine and fantasize. It is the essential home inside the home—a cell of self-sufficiency, a utopia for the self, or a *quant-à-soi* (personal preserve), according to Barthes. As beautiful as the idea might sound, the story that inspired Barthes's articulation of this idea is full of darkness and horror. It is the tale of a woman named Blanche Monnier, who was held captive by her own upper-middle-class family for almost twenty-five years, in a room behind closed shutters and doors, on a quiet beautiful street in the French town of Poitiers. The police found her emaciated and naked on a rotten straw mattress, surrounded by a blanket encrusted with excrement, scraps of old meat, fish, and bread, as well as insects and oyster shells. A heavy layer of dust lay in the room, and the floor had deteriorated. Her hair had never been cut, nor had her nails, and her head was wrapped inside the blanket, which she refused to take off. Written police accounts state that she resisted removal from her bed, referring to it as her "dear little grotto," giving it the affectionate and poetic name *mon cher grand fond Malampia* (my dear great dark Malampia). No one quite knows what she was referring to, but one can assume she had developed a deep sense of imagination and attachment to her space.

There are different ways to understand Blanche Monnier's behavior. One can assume there was physical abuse and emotional manipulation in the family prior to her confinement—her mother was blamed for her imprisonment. However, Barthes had a more controversial reading of the story. He suggested that no one knew whether she was forcibly confined, and that perhaps the mother had been condemned for complying with Blanche's own desire to retreat. The essence of Barthes's understanding was that Blanche had developed her own inner world where she felt protected and autonomous, unwilling to separate from anything (even her own waste) in an extreme strategy of resistance to any kind of loss, achieving what he called a *maison absolue*.

In times of crisis, we tend to idealize the home as a space of refuge and to project happiness onto the idea of retreating from the world. A famous French saying goes *pour être heureux, vivons cachés,* meaning, "to be happy, live in hiding." When discussing the German word *heimlich*, Freud pointed to its double signification of that which belongs to the house, is friendly and familiar, and of that which is concealed, or secret.[2] Having a room of one's own is an essential component of our development and growth, but over the course of the first year of the Covid-19 pandemic, many people—disproportionately women and children—were faced with the fact that their home was in fact the least safe space for them. Many horror films take place in domestic settings precisely because the experience of danger in a place that is meant to protect us may be the very definition of horror.

The accumulation of waste and decay in Blanche Monnier's room over twenty-five years could be understood through the lens of Julia Kristeva's *Powers of Horror: An Essay on Abjection*: "Fecal matter signifies,

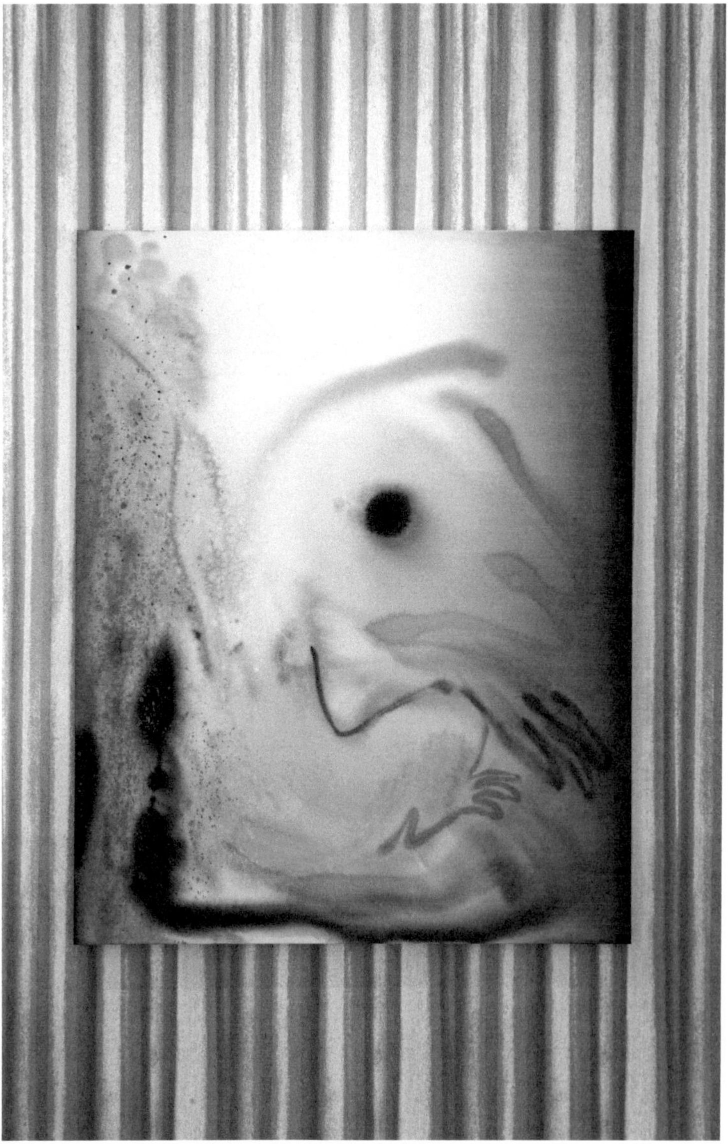

Yours Sincerely, 2022, Exhibition view, Mennour, *Le vers dans le fruit*, 2022

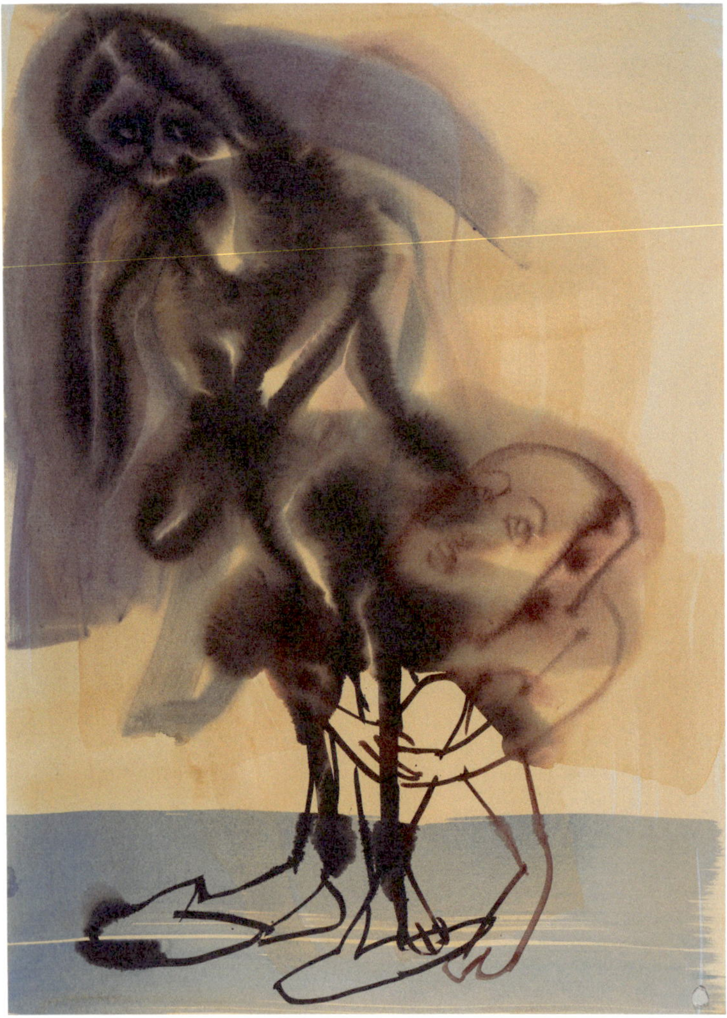

Un cri du coeur, 2019

as it were, what never ceases to separate from a body in a state of permanent loss in order to become autonomous, distinct from the mixtures, alternation, and decay that run through it.... Psychoanalysis has indeed seen that anal dejections constitute the first material separation that is controllable by the human being ... An operation that is dominated by the archaic idea of detachment and separation from the mother's body."[3] In a chapter of *How to Live Together* called "La Chambre" (The Room), Barthes said that the home is a projection of the body. But the reverse is also true: the first home we ever lived in *was* a body.[4]

The home-body is the hidden space beneath our bed sheets, our personal *maison absolue,* a warm and protective second skin. In a culture of transparency and constant exposure to social media, we reenact our search for the *maison absolue* when faced with a health crisis. We resist the contamination of the outside world and engage with a collective fantasy that Blanche Monnier also seemed to share: the desire to return to the womb and to undo the primal separation from the mother's body. The return to this space can be both desirable and frightening. In Iddu's favorite book, before the storm hits, Clarisse the mouse wonders if the wind will uproot her home, and she can't decide whether she would prefer for the house to stay in place or to be whisked away.

1 Roland Barthes, *How To Live Together* (New York, 2002), p. 49.
2 Sigmund Freud, *Das Umheimliche* (1919) (Ditzingen, 2020), p. 9.
3 Julia Kristeva, *Powers of Horror: An Essay on Abjection* (New York, 1982), p. 108.
4 Barthes 2002 (see note 1), p. 61.

After School

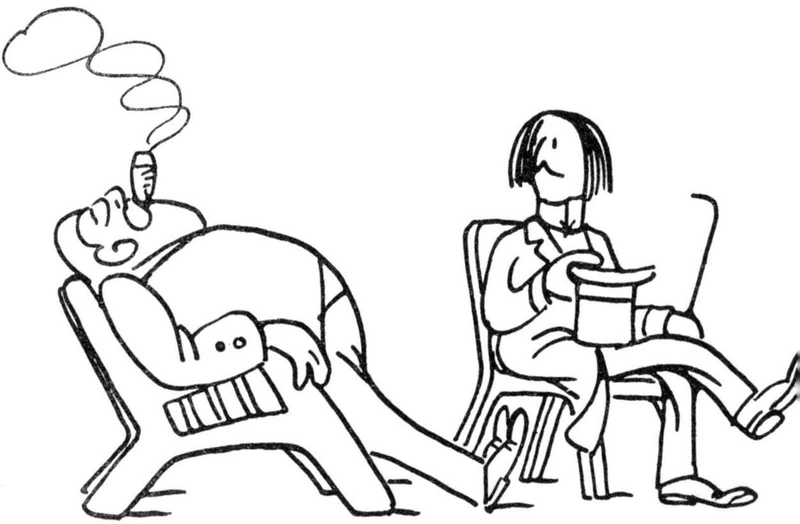

Cartoon by André Hellé in the magazine
La Petite Caricature. Journal de contes joyeux

When I was pregnant, I turned into an entitled bourgeois man. I wore oversize men's shirts and jackets, and started to take up more and more physical space. Sitting on the New York City subway, I would arrange my legs in such a way that some would call manspreading. Like an affluent, deep-pocketed character from a nineteenth-century novel, I carried my big belly like a sign of opulence and prestige, walking slowly and expecting people to move out of my way. Even my shortness of breath made me feel like I had smoked too many expensive cigars.

Obviously, this experience of pregnancy didn't relate much to the expectations that I had internalized, being born female and socialized as a woman. Like Louise Bourgeois, I thought for a long time that I would be unable to have a child—doctors had instilled a fear in me that I was too thin, and then too old. Like Louise, I grew up with the knowledge that my parents would have preferred a son and gave me a feminine version of a boy's name. I was so convinced that I would be infertile that I grew to resent the image of the pregnant woman. I made a drawing of a pregnant woman as an entitled, perfectionist dancer, defying gravity and ejaculating from the joy of her own performance in *Feeling Good*. I gave her the face of Nathalie Portman in Darren Aronofsky's film *Black Swan*. In the end, the doctors were wrong about my ability to conceive, and I quickly discovered that I was also wrong about the pregnant body's ability to defy gravity. But I was right about one aspect: the dysmorphic dissociation. The reality of pregnancy is actually as fracturing for the psyche as Aronofsky's paranoiac tale.

Pregnancy is widely understood as the ultimate marker of femininity, but during gestation the ambiguity of gender is far more present. In my eighteen months of pregnancy, I have carried two penises in my womb and felt a new form of empathy toward the male sex. It may also be that my disgust at the societal expectations of "mothers" and the inherent devalorization of this figure made it more attractive for me to identify with men. The increasing commercialization and artificiality of the institution of "motherhood," its sugar-coated aesthetic in social media culture, the weight of domestic duties, and the narcissistic reward were not what I wanted for myself.

Maggie Nelson expressed some similar thoughts on gender fluidity and anxiety in her brilliant book *The Argonauts*. In the book, Nelson recounts the experience of her pregnancy at the same time as her partner, artist Harry Dodge, was undergoing a gender transition. Maggie becomes pregnant through in-vitro fertilization and together they form their own version of a nuclear family for whom queerness is not a concept but simply an experience of life. I believe Nelson's book should be a part of every academic and medical school curriculum in order to challenge common ways of thinking about pregnancy and gender identity.

Catherine Clément, in the first part of *La Jeune Née* (The Newly Born Woman), writes that pregnancy and gender transition were often associated with one another and celebrated in traditional cultures as being spectacular transformative processes of the body, but were later influenced and subjected to more restrictive taboos and rules.[1] The lesson you learn when becoming a parent is essentially that bodies have no stable form or identity, but instead are just a vehicle

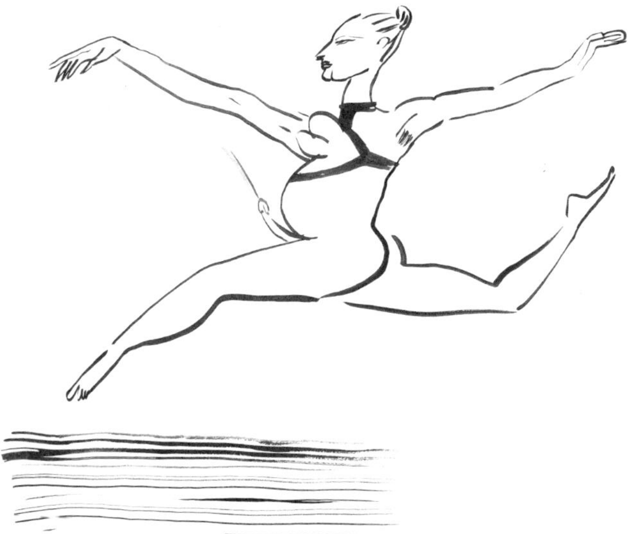

Feeling Good II, 2015

for relating to others. A child grows, uteruses blow up and contract, everything changes, moves, falls. All the clothes in your closet seem to belong to someone else all of a sudden—nothing fits for long, in any case. The impermanence and dissolution of identity are among some of the most obvious lessons of maternity. Gender, and even the relationship between mother and child, would be better defined by degree than by essence, fluctuating under the influence of hormones and the passage of time.

One day I called my son a "little boy," and he screamed at me "NOOOOO!" I asked, "What are you then?" to which he simply replied, "I'm a dog." Identifying with an animal is, for children, as natural as identifying with the mother, the father, or anything that catches their attention and empathy. Interspecies self-identification may be a good way to protect children from the heaviness of gender prejudice—and from losing their inborn ability to associate and identify with multiple references under the pressure of a heteronormative environment. Children's books make good use of this trope, perhaps in part for that very reason.

Every parent with enough empathy and curiosity for their own child's development should agree that heteronormativity is a restrictive cultural construct, and that dismantling it should not fall on the LGBTQIA2S+ community alone. Nuances in gender and the difference between sexual and gender identity should not be treated as an exception to the norm: they are the very origin of our psychological and natural beings. French child psychiatrist Luiz Alvarez refers to Sigmund Freud's view on bisexuality.

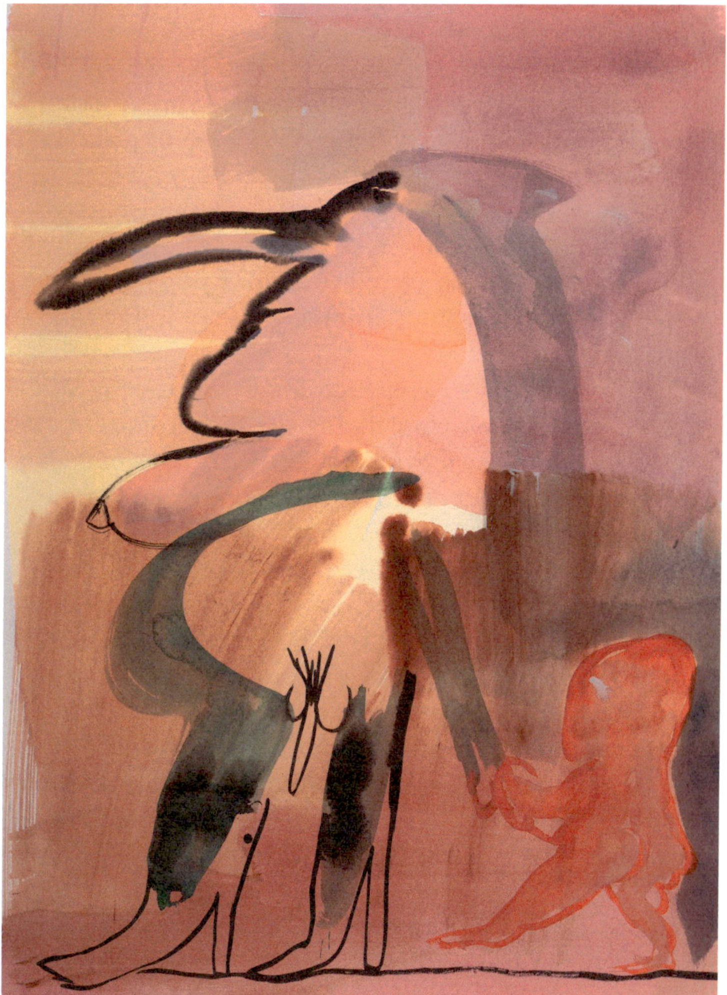

After School, 2019

Between the ages of three and five, children of both sexes explore what it would be like to be either a boy or a girl, depending on what they want and need to be. At this time, all children believe they can both have a penis and carry a baby in their belly. The temperament of a firstborn child when their mother is pregnant with a new baby is not one of jealousy (that comes later), but rather "belly envy," which is as common as "penis envy," but far less discussed. Children may also express a wonderfully creative fluidity of gender on their own terms when traditional gender roles are not reinforced in their homes and social environments.

The drawing *After School* (2019) refers to the process of unlearning and challenging the dichotomies and paradoxes that society has established. Tales of gods giving birth to children and saints drinking milk from animals have long existed. Zeus, for example, swallowed his pregnant wife Metis and was literally pregnant with their child Athena, who was eventually born from his skull. This story could be considered a male appropriation of pregnancy, but revisiting it through an alternative lens may allow us to think about it as a narrative of shared responsibilities.

The filmmaker Ala Eddine Slim brings this story to a more contemporary setting in his 2019 film *Tlamess*. A soldier escapes the Tunisian military to live as a hermit in a cave hidden by bushes. Hair grows on his body and he progressively loses the ability to speak, living in separation from the human world. Parallel to this storyline, a pregnant woman in a seemingly perfect marriage to a wealthy man is seen roaming her luxurious home and garden in a state of melancholy. While talking in the woods, she encounters the soldier, faints, and later finds herself in his cave. Together, they await the birth of the child, and in a magical scene, the two switch gender roles in an instant. The baby cries loudly to be fed, but the mother has no milk to give. She throws the reclusive soldier a desperate glance, and he begins to produce milk from his own breast and satiates the crying child.

As provocative and unlikely as this scene may seem, male lactation is not entirely illogical—men possess nipples, after all, and induced milk production in a nonpregnant partner as well as trans women is well documented. Miraculous male lactation appears in the Talmud, and anecdotally in Leo Tolstoy's *Anna Karenina*. Charles Darwin speculated that all humans once nursed young, and male goats and some bats have been observed to lactate in times of stress or need. Like gender and milk, the capacity to care is fluid.

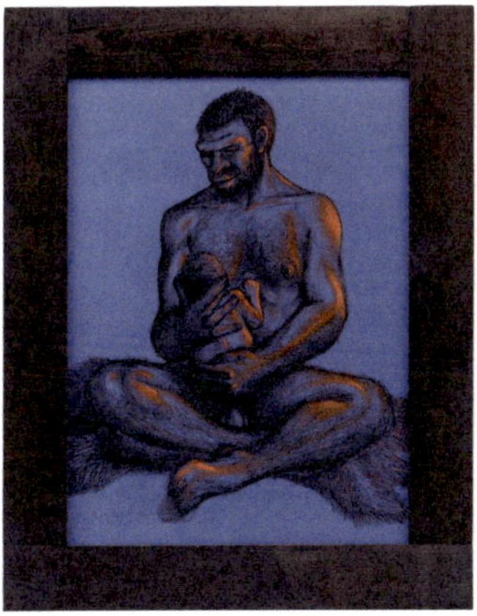

Homo Homo Neanderthalensis (Breastfeeding Daddy), Rasmus Myrup, 2020

1 Catherine B. Clément, "Premiere Partie: La Coupable," in Catherine B. Clément and Hélène Cixous, *La Jeune Née* (Paris, 1975), pp. 7–113.

The Disorder of Things

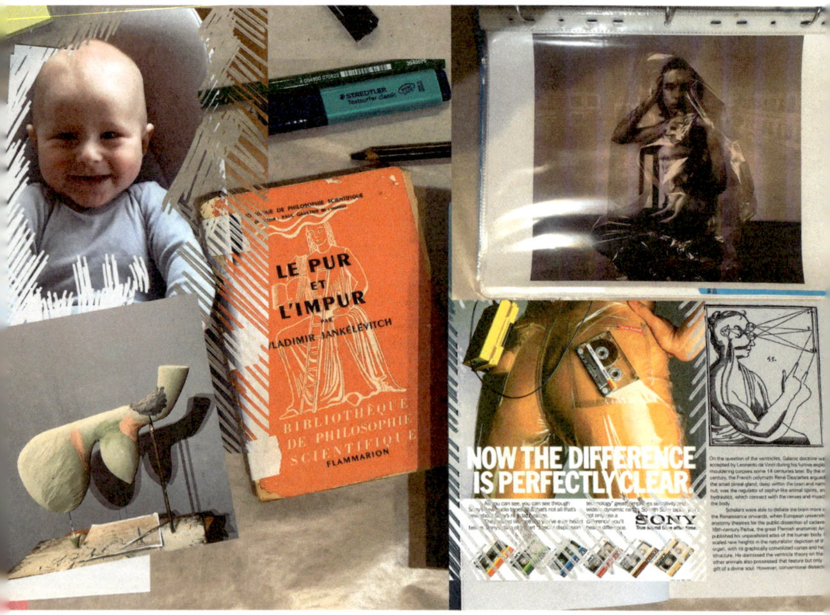

Digital collage of personal photos, an image of the model for the bronze sculpture *Learning to Loose*, the book *Le Pur et L'impur*, a Sony advertisement, and other reference images.

Less is more. I've been given this advice several times in my life. For a child, though, more is more—more toys, more stories, more episodes of *PAW Patrol*, more playtime, more cuddles. The ability to set limits, to understand our own hierarchy of desires, and to accept frustration are important aspects of our transition into adulthood.

When it comes to collecting images, I feel I am still far from my coming of age. The references I amass consistently overload the storage capacity of my phone and computer and overflow from binders and notebooks on my desk. Fragments of museum catalogues, novels, screenshots of Instagram posts, excerpts from poems, essays, Google Image searches, objects, and fragments of conversations I hear on my walks through New York City's Chinatown all make their way into my collection. Part of me believes that by overaccumulating, I introduce the possibility of randomness. When my range of references is wide enough, when I'm not too focused on finding one thing, then my selection and reasoning turns into a series of clues, an investigation. I trust intuition and the human brain's wonderful ability to make connections, and find differences between things.

In 2016, I did a writing project of responses to spam emails with my friend and frequent collaborator, the poet Jacob Bromberg. The project resulted in the installation *Office of Unreplied Emails* (2016). One particular response to Groupon, a discount e-commerce marketplace, comes to mind: "Dear Groupon, I feel like a wild rabbit hunted by possibility, like the prey of all worlds." Is the excess of things an escapist strategy to avoid decision-making?

Biologically, we all lean toward a need for stimulation and satiation, like a moth to a light at night or a fruit fly to some sweet juice on the kitchen countertop. When I'm about to draw, I like to eat something sweet, put my music playlists on really loud, and maniacally sift through my reference images. The references are like a drug that excites me—I feel high on the images and sounds. It's when I'm close to overdose that I know it's time to get to work.

Currently on my virtual and physical desktops:

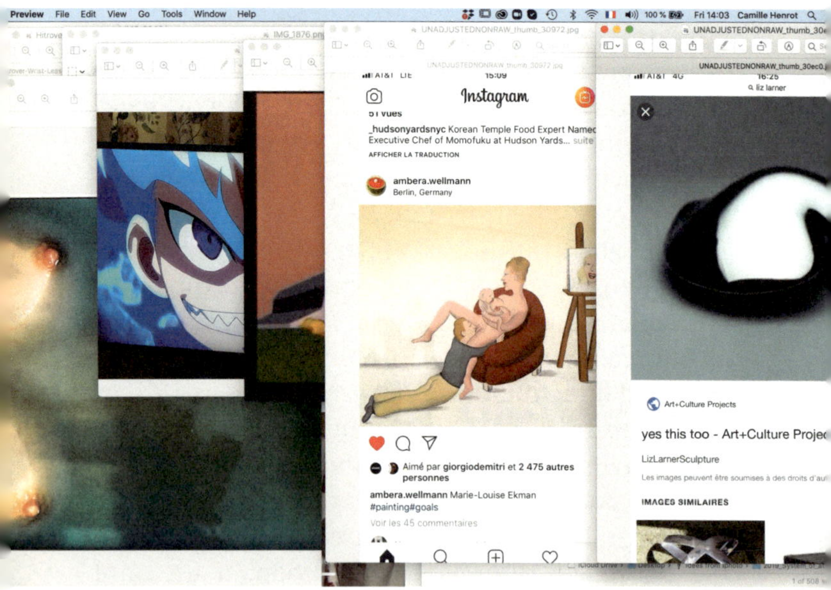

Image from the book *Masters of Erotic Photography*, a Manga cartoon character, Instagram screenshot (@ambera.wellmann) of a painting by Marie Louise Ekman, a screenshot of a sculpture by Liz Larner.

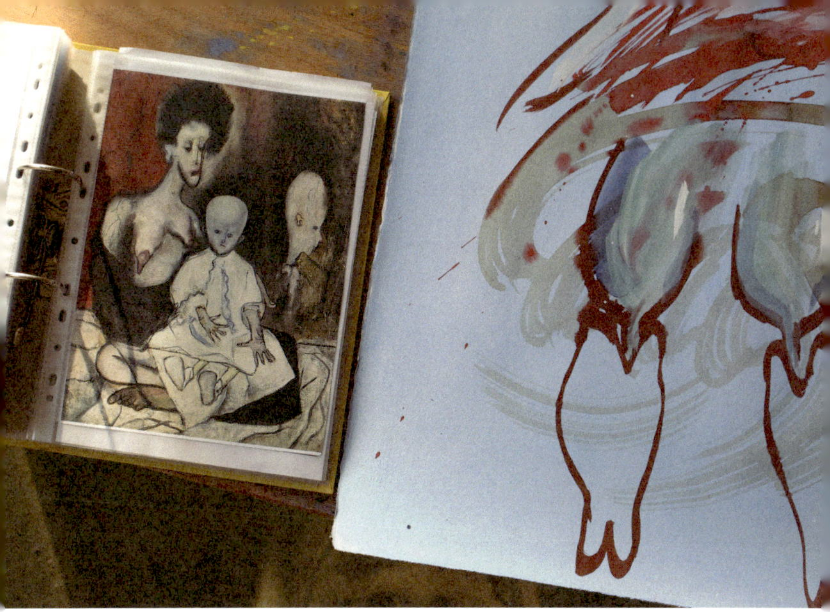

My drawing next to my binder of reference images,
displaying Alice Neel's painting *Degenerate Madonna* (1930).

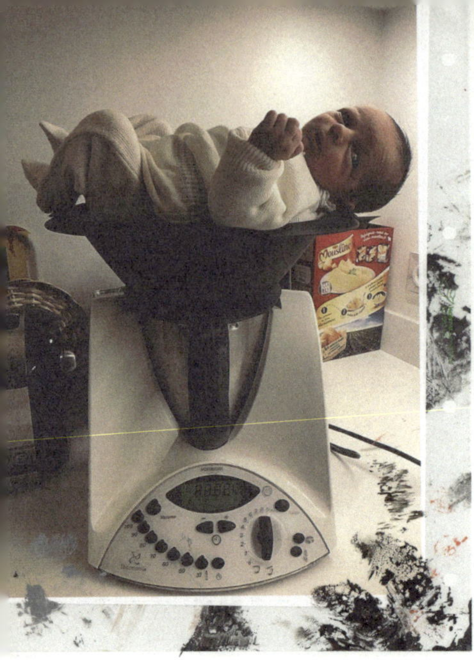

Printed photo of my nephew being weighed at one week old on a kitchen scale, taken by my sister Mathilde Henrot-Raja, from my binder of reference images for the series *System of Attachment* (2019–21).

Below (clockwise from top left): Printed black-and-white image of Kitagawa Utamaro's print *Pearl Divers* (1802–06), cartoon by Tex Avery, René Girard's *Géométrie du désir*, Instagram screenshots, photo from Lisa Sorigni's series *Behind Glass* (2020), unknown stone sculpture, Wilhelm Reich's book *The Bioelectric Investigation of Sexuality and Anxiety* (1981).

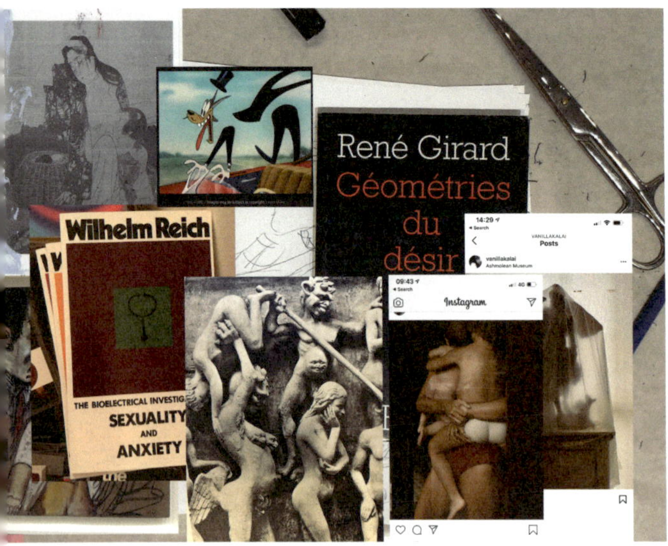

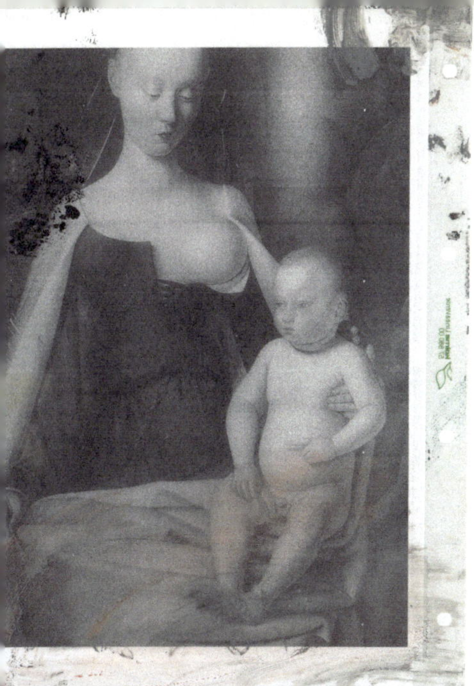

Printed black-and-white detail of Jean Fouquet's *Melun Diptych* (1450), left panel only. From my binder of reference images for the series *System of Attachment* (2019–21).

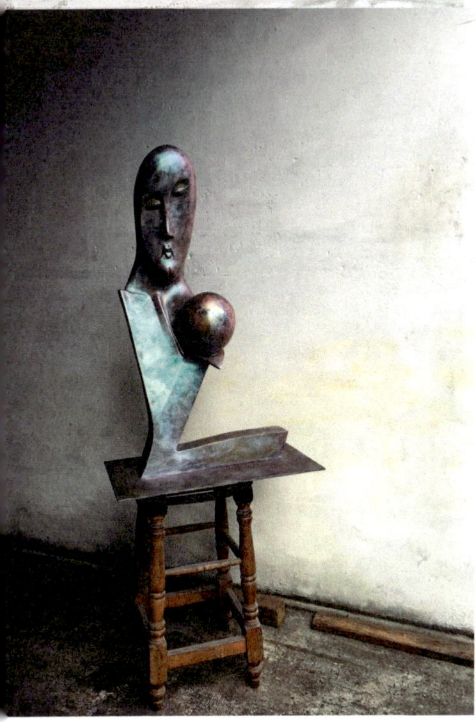

Y Woman, 2021, bronze work in production at Atelier Milome, Romainville, France.

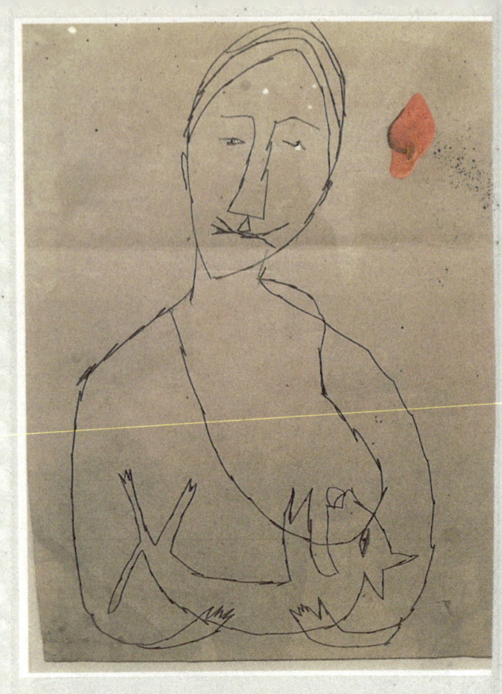

Printed image of Andy Warhol's drawing *Female with Animal at Breast*, ca. 1948–49. From my binder of reference images for the series *System of Attachment* (2019–21).

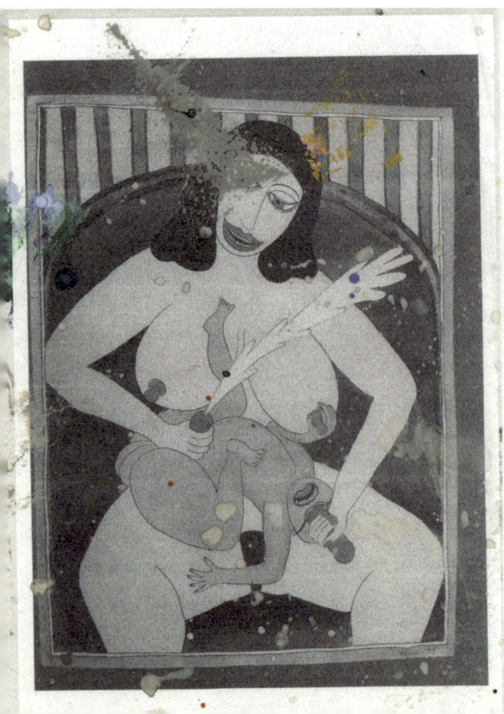

Printed black-and-white image of a painting by Hans Schärer *Ohne Titel (Untitled)* (1977).

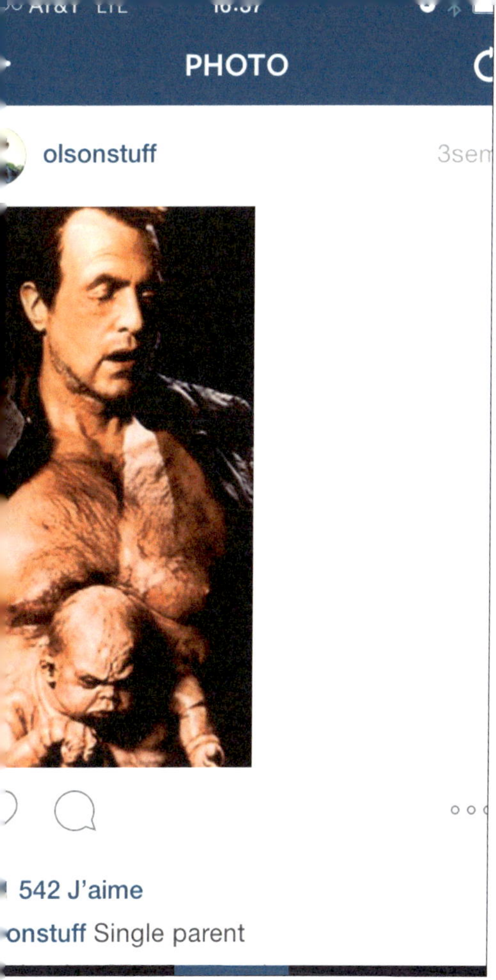

Instagram screenshot (@olsonstuff) of a man pregnant with an angry child.

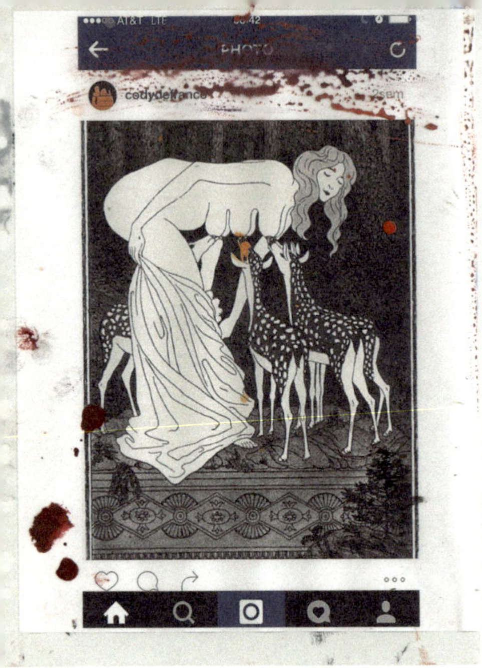

Printed image of Instagram screenshot (@corydefranco) of Thomas Theodor Heine's illustration *Genevieve* (1911). From my binder of reference images for the series *System of Attachment* (2019–21).

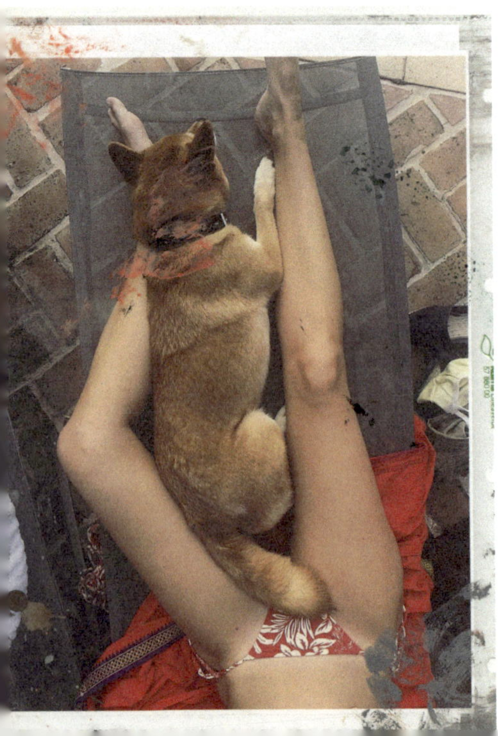

Personal photo from my binder of reference images for the series *System of Attachment* (2019–21).

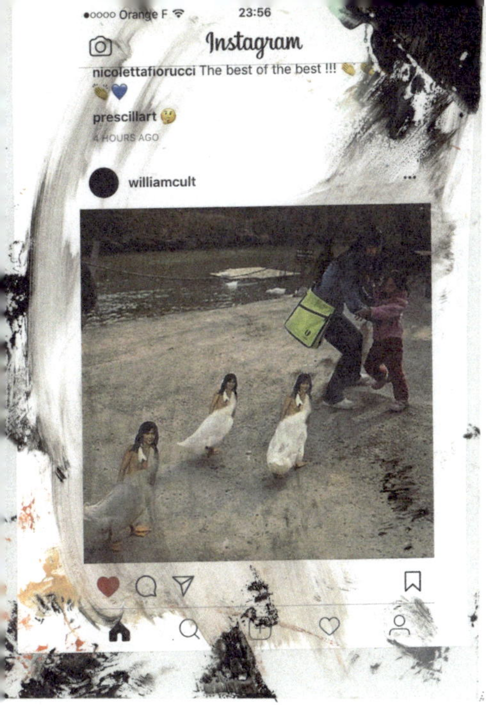

Printed image of Instagram screenshot (@williamcult) of a woman and child running from three swans whose upper bodies have the form of Björk in her iconic swan gown. From my binder of reference images for the series *System of Attachment* (2019–21).

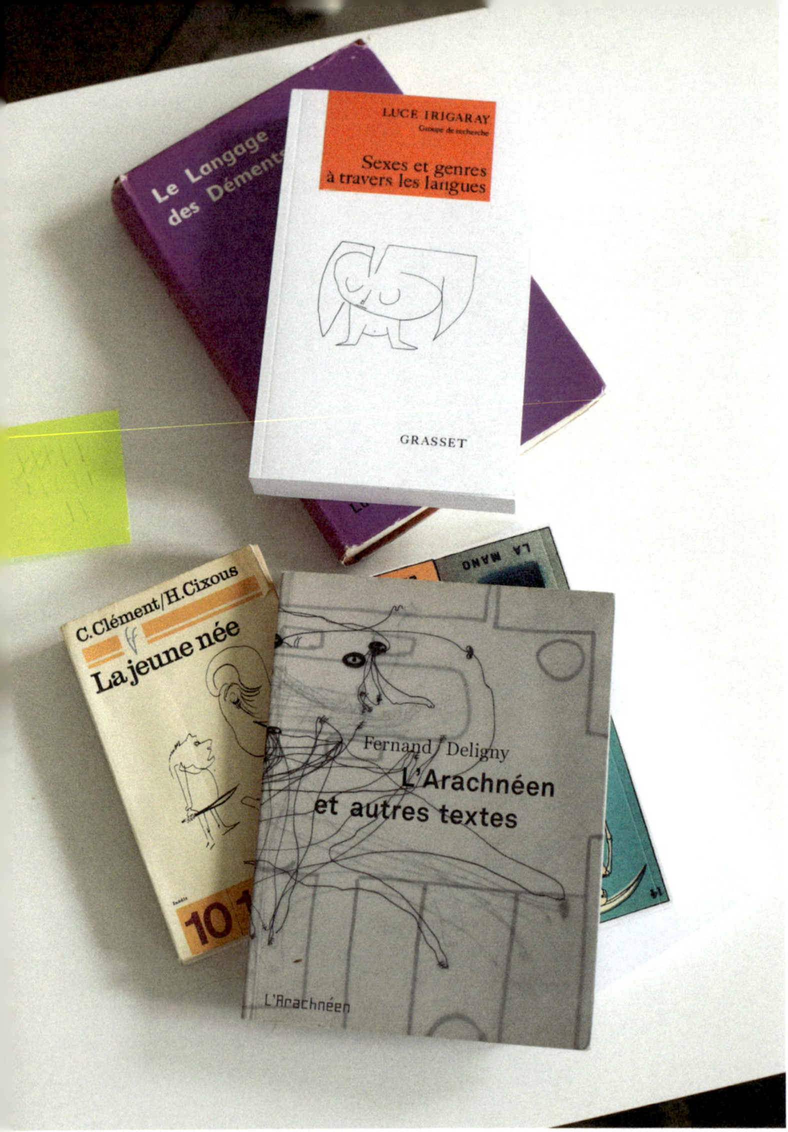

Books on my desk during
residency at Callie's Berlin, 2021

List of Books

— *Mother Reader* edited by Moyra Davey, with contributions by Susan Griffin, Ursula K. Le Guin, Doris Lessing, Toni Morrison, Sylvia Platz, Adrienne Rich, among others, 2001
— *Le langage des déments*, 1973, *Ce sexe qui n'en est pas un*, 1977, and *Être deux*, 1997, by Luce Irigaray
— *Men and Apparitions* by Lynne Tillman, 2018
— *Un appartement sur Uranus* by Paul B. Preciado, 2019
— *The Republic of Motherhood* by Liz Berry, 2018
— *La jeune née* by Hélène Cixous, Catherine Clement, and the illustrator Mechtilt, 1975
— *The Arachnean and Other Texts*, by Fernand Deligny 2015
— *La difficulté de vivre: Le psychanalyste et la prévention des névroses* by Françoise Dolto
— *Inside the Blood Factory* by Diane Wakoski, 1968
— *Fantasmatic interaction and intergenerational transmission* by Serge Lebovici, 1988
— *Caliban And The Witch: Women, The Body, and Primitive Accumulation* by Silvia Federici, 2004
— *Motherhood* by Sheila Heti, 2018
— *Comment vivre ensemble: Cours et séminaires au Collège de France* (1976–77), by Roland Barthes, 2002
— *Portrait du soleil* by Hélène Cixous, 1974
— *Patriarchy Stress Disorder: The Invisible Inner Barrier to Women's Happiness and Fulfillment* by Valerie Rein, 2019
— *Wet: On Painting, Feminism and Art Culture* by Mira Schor, 1997
— *The Left Hand of Darkness* by Ursula K. Le Guin, 1969

— *Uncut Funk: A Contemplative Dialogue* by bell hooks and Stuart Hall, 2018
— *And Nanny Makes Three* by Jessika Auerbach, 2007

List of Songs

— "No G.D.M.," Gina X Performance
— "Running Out of Time," Rexy
— "Little Raver," Superpitcher
— "Queen of the Minstrels," Mr. Day
— "Invitation," Saâda Bonaire
— "Wawa by the Ocean," Mary Lattimore
— "Aht Uh Mi Hed," Shuggie Otis
— "Synthesize Me," The Space Lady
— "I Go To Sleep," The Kinks
— "Camille," Ana Roxane
— "You Could Be More as You Are," Saâda Bonaire
— "All of a Sudden," Laraaji
— "Sinzo No Tobira," Utaka No Hibi
— "Get Around to It," Arthur Russell
— "Everybody's Gotta Live," Love
— "The Combine," John Maus
— "Didn't I," Darondo
— "Sweet Surrender," Tim Buckley
— "Extremely Bad Man," Shintaro Sakamoto
— "October (Love Song)," Chris & Cosey
— "Nowhere Near," Yo La Tengo
— "Licking an Orchid," Yves Tumor
— "Baby Please Don't Go," Rose Mitchell
— "Some Things Last a Long Time," Daniel Johnston
— "These Days," Nico
— "Momo's," Connan Mockasin
— "The Narcissist," Dean Blunt

— "Make Me Tea," Woo
— "Space Talk," Asha Puthli
— "Umi No Ue Kara," Yasuaki Shimizu
— "In Every Dream Home a Heartache," Roxy Music
— "Why Can't There Be Love?," Dee Edwards
— "O Superman," Laurie Anderson
— "A Cry for Love," The Black Heart Procession
— "Dream Baby Dream," Suicide
— "Day Is Done," Nick Drake
— "My Sister," Tinderstick
— "Cet enfant que je t'avais fait," Brigitte Fontaine
— "Melocoton," Colette Magny
— "Bela Lugosi's Dead," Bauhaus
— "This Lullaby," Queens of the Stone Age
— "Lungomare," Lust for Youth
— "Saint," Blood Orange

Pump and Dump

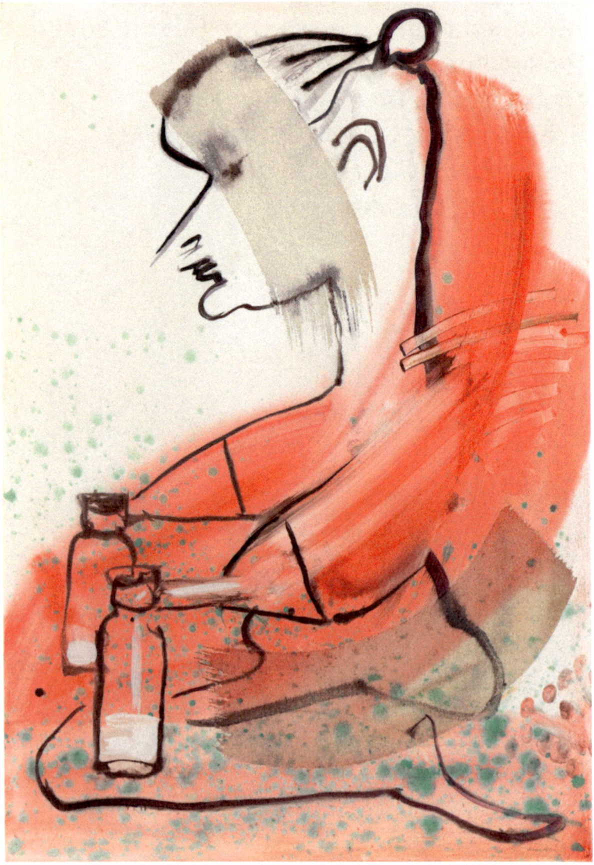

Expressioning, 2020

And still the labour of mothers is unpaid.
– Susan Griffin[1]

Being a mother is a relational role, and there are scant few representations of the mother as a subject independent from her child. In all the books I've read about raising children, the mother is never dissociated from the child and so never dissociated from the gaze that turns her into an object or attribute of the child—her existence is predicated on that of the child. This act of erasure and my own experience of it as a tacit societal demand to disappear made me want to dedicate a series of works to the breast pump, which seems to give rise to the only situation where the woman as mother appears on her own as a full human being while maintaining a nurturing role.

In 2019, I asked my friend Jenny Schlenzka, now director of Gropius Bau, who had recently given birth to her second child, if she would be willing to model for me. I had forgotten the positions involved in the process of pumping milk: where the hands should go, how the body should relax in order to be comfortable. She agreed, and some time before coming to sit for me as she pumped milk, she sent me a photo of a passage from Maggie Nelson's masterpiece *The Argonauts*: "Beyond photographs in breast pump manuals (and lactation porn), [...] images of milk expression are really nowhere to be found. Phrases such as colostrum, letdown, and hindmilk arrive in one's life like hieroglyphs from the land of the lost."[2]

This excerpt opened a new horizon in my mind, sparking an association between lactation and masturbation. The association began with the taboo around these natural acts, but deepened when I thought about how Michel Leiris, in *Phantom Africa*, writes about the satisfaction, lust, and waste of masturbation when his sperm splashes to the ground.[3] Perhaps the experience of the loss and relief of milk dripping or squirting out of the nipple could be described similarly.

Lactation can create a sensual, not quite sexual pleasure from the feeling of the breast being emptied, relieved of the tension and the weight of the milk within as it is stimulated by the child's suckling.

But while nursing can be a deeply pleasurable experience on a number of levels, lactating with a breast pump—a machine invented to avoid the loss of milk—provokes a sense of inadequacy, guilt, and shame: another parallel with masturbation. Unlike the titillating guilt of masturbation, though, the guilt of the purely utilitarian breast pump is pleasureless. The breast pump itself is a bit painful, and the mechanical breathing of the machine is so close to the sound of milking machines for cows that it is sometimes hard to dissociate the two. It clearly was not made for the mother so much as for society *through* the mother. The machine allows you to go "hands free," but still very much fixes you in place and makes it impossible to do much more than wait for the milk to drip out of your body, drop by drop.

As my body and the machine become one big nourishment apparatus, my head begins ruminating, asking monkey-mind questions. What does it mean that women are the first food? Is the machine a robotic baby? Could its music be a good synth-like base for a contemporary musical composition? Why are images of breasts leaking milk nowhere to be found, but boobs are everywhere? What if I were encouraged by the machine and decided to give myself over even more to the baby, letting my job fall to the wayside? Is artistic practice a job? Is nursing a job?

Milk makers are breadwinners, but when they produce milk, their loaves get sliced. Elizabeth Caucutt's study "Why Do Women Wait?" shows "workers that postpone motherhood experience increased earnings, but upon the event of motherhood, endure sustained wage flattening. This wage penalty is amplified among women of higher education levels, resulting in fewer labor interruptions (children) due to the cost of maternity leave on future earnings and the absence of paid parental leave policies in the US."[4 5]

On the website of OASH, the Office on Women's Health from the US Department of Health & Human Services, I found a list of recommendations for employers who find themselves with breastfeeding female employees.[6] Besides making sure to offer an adequate accommodation, a "lactation space" like a separate room with a comfortable chair and magazines (as if reading a magazine on the side were an option while nursing a baby), they are told to make sure to give them a "break," yet they are not obligated to compensate for it: "If extra time is needed because a mother is pumping or expressing milk," it says, "that extra time can be unpaid." Both notions—to consider milk pumping as a "break"—and not paying for it, should be reasons enough to swamp the Department of Health & Human Services with letters of protest.

The breast pump is an ambivalent tool of independence and alienation. It reveals the conflictual expectation pressed upon breastfeeding women to be in two places at once—nursing while they are working

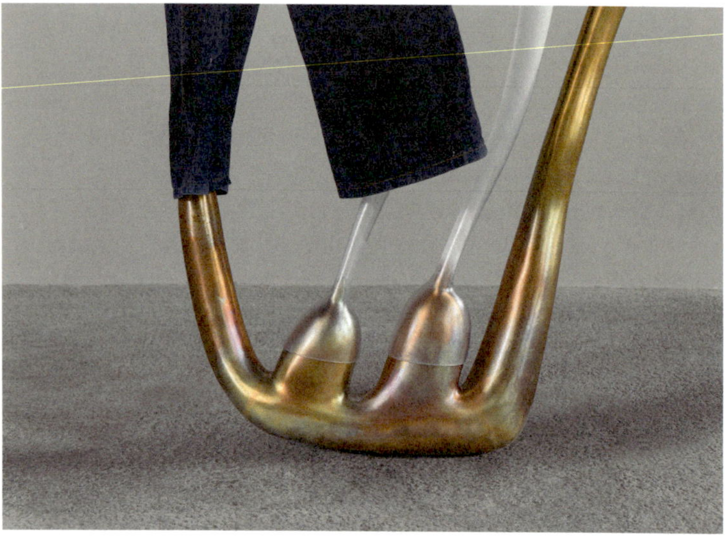

End of Me, 2021

and working while they are nursing. At the same time, it also often acts as a goad for the mother to submit to a quantified production that casts women as resources to be exploited. It enslaves the mother as it serves her, becoming the ultimate symbol of both the commodification of the female body and her working efforts. The breast pump embodies the highest contradictory demands in biotechnocapitalism as it maintains the illusion that the opposition between capitalist society and human health can be resolved by technology. It can't.

End of Me (2021) was born out of an attempt to translate my meditations on the breast pump into a sculpture. It evokes a body that has escaped from its clothes, or a body sucked up or liquified in its totality by the breast pump. There is only one character feeding from itself here, but it is also emptying itself, in a sort of self-sacrifice or self-building: it both nourishes and gives of itself, like a kind of phoenix. Silvia Federici recently highlighted the nauseating irony in the fact that for decades feminists have had to fight for the choice to not have a child, and now we must also contend with increasingly difficult financial hurdles to have one if a child *is* desired.[7] We live in a strange time and society where the demanding labor of waking up every three hours at night to nurse and then to connect yourself to a machine, sitting on the toilet waiting for your milk to be extracted, is actually a privilege not everyone can afford.

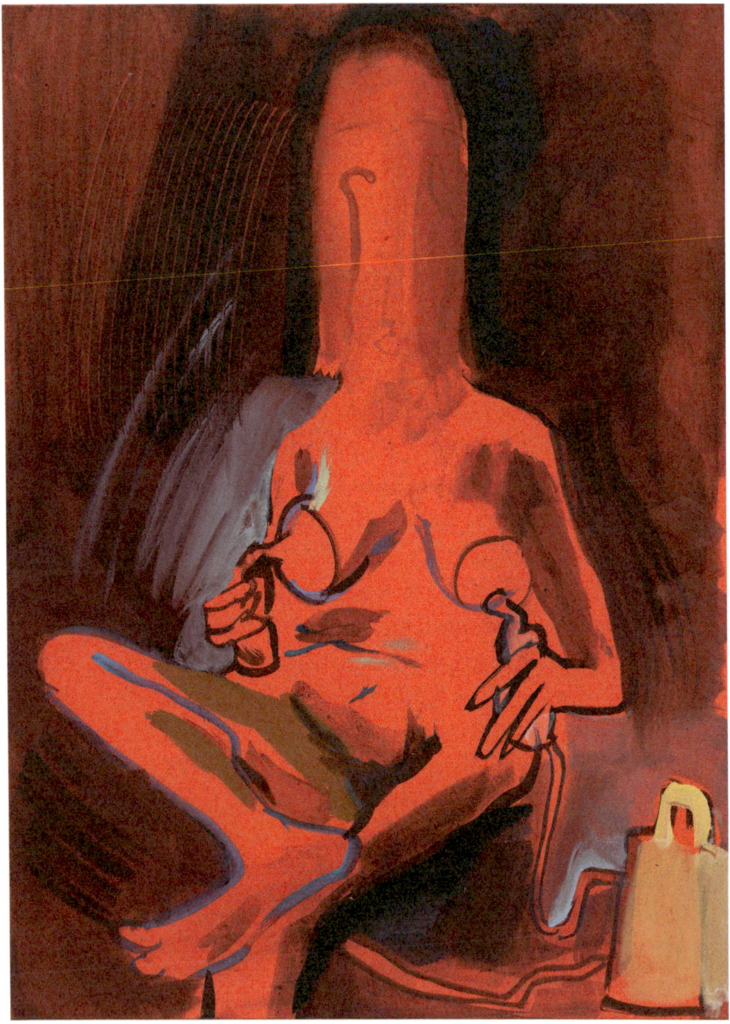

Wet Job, 2020

1 Susan Griffin, “Feminism and Motherhood,” 1974, in Moyra Davey, ed. *Mother Reader: Essential Writings about Motherhood* (New York, 2001), p. 40.
2 Maggie Nelson. *The Argonauts* (Minneapolis, 2015), p. 115.
3 Michel Leiris, *L'Afrique Fantome* (Paris, 1934), p. 244.
4 Kealey Boyd, “The Very Real ‘Motherhood Penalty’ in the Art World,” Cecilia Dan Fine Art (website), May 21, 2021, https://www.ceciliadan.com/blog/the-very-real-motherhood-penalty-in-the-art-world (accessed March 18, 2023).
5 Elizabeth M. Caucutt et. al, “Why Do Women Wait? Matching, Wage Inequality, and the Incentives for Fertility Delay,” in *Review of Economic Dynamics* (2002), 5(4), pp. 815–55.
6 “What Employers Need to Know,” US Women's Health website, https://www.womenshealth.gov/supporting-nursing-moms-work/what-law-says-about-breastfeeding-and-work/what-employers-need-know (accessed March 18, 2023).
7 Valentine Faure, “Notre corps est un réservoir de savoir-faire, de résistances,” *Le Monde*, July 17, 2021, https://www.lemonde.fr/series-d-ete/article/2021/07/17/notre-corps-est-un-reservoir-de-savoir-faire-de-resistances_6088553_3451060.html (accessed March 18, 2023).

Milk: On Debt

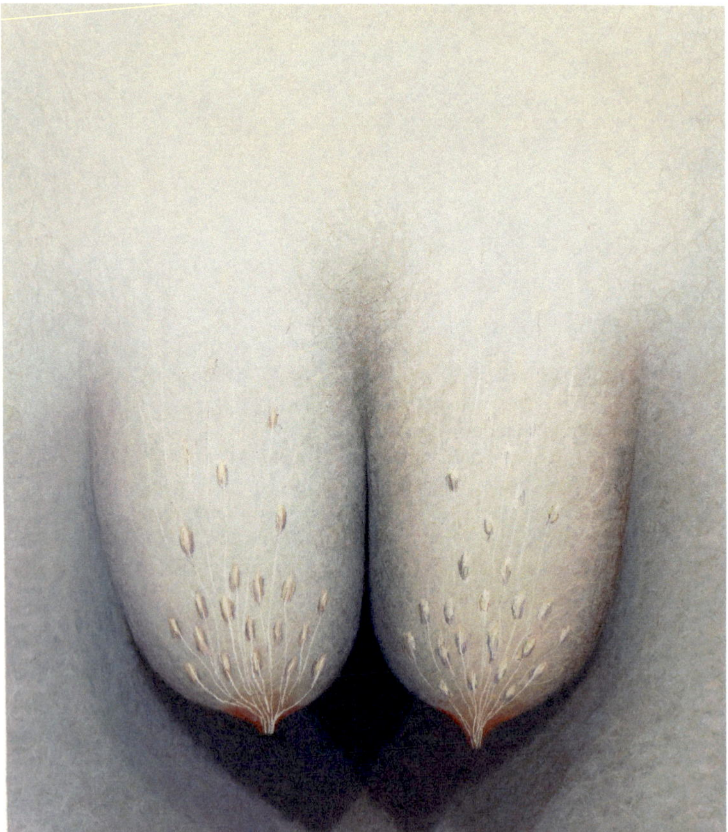

Loie Hollowell, *Engorgement*, 2021

It took me a while to compile and pare down my notes and actually start writing about mother's milk. There's something about this liquid produced by our own bodies that's difficult to contain. It just spills out in all directions. Writing about milk is a bit like writing with white ink—ideas are hatched and then reabsorbed into the larger picture, making it hard to tell where the subject begins and where it ends. How and where can milk be kept from spreading indefinitely? In the breast? In the mother? In the child?

As a French person with a newborn in the United States, I was perplexed when I first heard the word "express" used in relation to breastfeeding. There is a strange beauty mixed with the shame of this puritanical euphemism for squeezing milk out of your breast to stimulate milk production. It made me ask myself, if milk could express itself—if it could speak—what would it have to say?

All bodily fluids—semen, blood, sweat, urine—carry different highly debated and contested connotations. But none of these is associated with the sense of innocence and purity that milk often evokes in people's minds. The mother-child bond certainly has a lot to do with this, but so too does the liquid's color—wrapped up with its own complicated connotations.

At a time when nursing children was still considered a job that could be executed by any woman, milk became the battleground for the most atrocious forms of gender, class, and racial discrimination. Over centuries, enslaved Black mothers were forced to breastfeed white children to the detriment of their own children's health. In mid-nineteenth-century France, a great number of newborns were entrusted

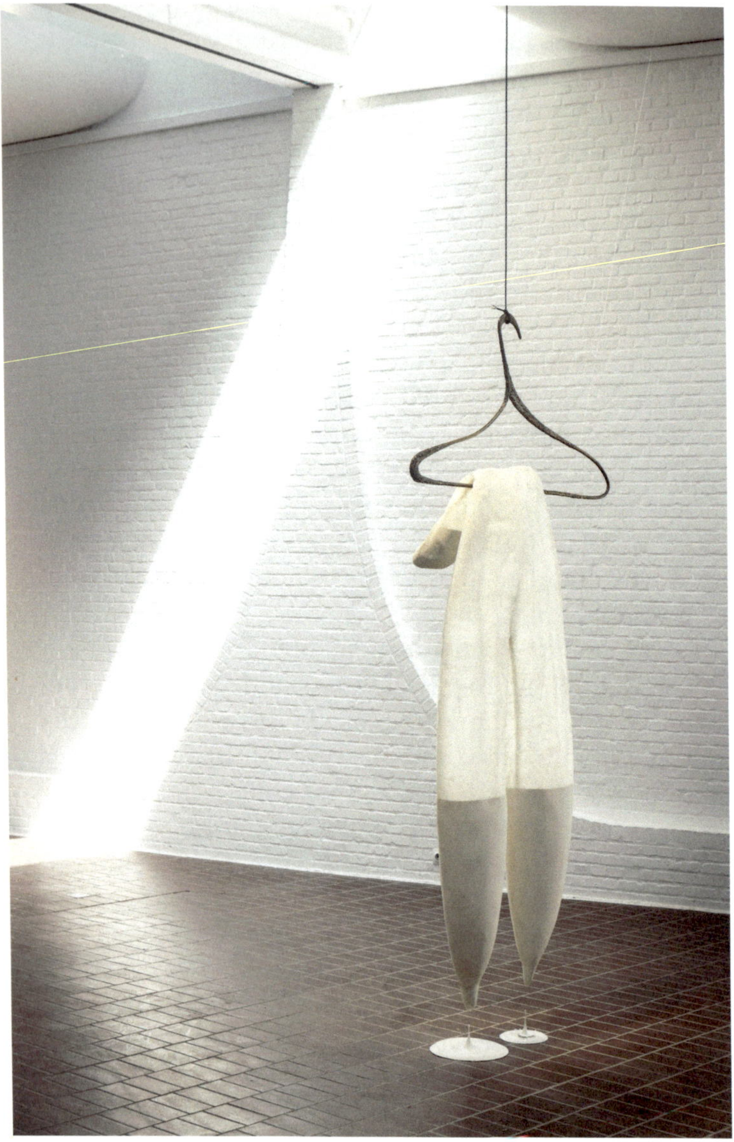

A Free Quote, 2021, Exhibition view, Middelheim Museum, *Wet Job*, 2022

to "mercenary" wet nurses because their families were too poor to allow mothers to abstain from paid work. A majority of these children died, because the nurses—at the end of an economic chain of impoverished women—often took on more children than they could physically feed. At the same time, as Paul B. Preciado writes in *An Apartment on Uranus*, scientists such as Carl Linnaeus shunned the role of the wet nurse, theorizing that the exchange of bodily fluids created racial and class contaminations.[1] The term "white blood" was coined to describe "the milk of a sexually active woman" and "deemed responsible for a child's death," while a study conducted by Agnès Fine in villages in the Pyrenees found a belief in the transference of strong emotions via breast milk, still widely held circa 1980, called *lait trouble*, or murky/troubled milk. Even today, when most of the aforementioned myths seem to be banned from institutionalized guidance on breastfeeding, you find organizations that fetishize breast milk to an extent that turns it into the holy grail of infant nutrition. "I AM THE MILK OF YOUR BREASTS. YOU SHALL HAVE NO OTHER FORM OF INFANT NUTRITION IN YOUR HOUSE"[2] reads a commandment issued online by one of the numerous groups that constitute the radical breastfeeding movement epitomized by La Leche League. While it is true that breast milk protects the child from diseases (similar to vaccines, as the World Health Organization asserts), imagine the pressure and fear of all those parents in these pandemic times who cannot or don't want to breastfeed their baby—an anxiety that was exacerbated by the shortage of baby formula in 2022.

On a website called *Only the Breast*, which serves as an online marketplace for women who want to buy, sell, or donate breast milk, I found the questions: "Are you overproducing and want to list your liquid gold for sale?" and "Looking to make a few extra bucks while clearing out your freezer?" The images were novel, but the underlying thoughts struck me as unsurprising—that breast milk is considered to be metaphorically worth its weight in gold and that women are held to the standard of clean kitchens. Breastfeeding is subject to a never-ending circle of performance and productivity that shuts out the psychological and physiological mess it leaves behind. I will never forget the amount of shame that I was overdosed with in the US when I did not produce enough milk. There is a value *per se* in quantity and overproduction at the expense of women's well-being.

Breastfeeding changed my perception of milk. When it spills all over the place it leaves yellow stains on your clothes that are among the most stubborn spots to remove. Milk is sticky, and once I forgot a milliliter or two on the table in my studio. After a few days it smelled so bad I was ready to vomit. All of which shows how close the categories of the sacred and disgust really are.

"And yet the body *in extremis*—the body experiencing itself acutely as a body—as a human reality to which mothers cannot help but have access, although once again they are expected to put a lid on it, to make everything sweet and nice," Jacqueline Rose writes in *Mothers: An Essay on Love and Cruelty*.[3] "They can, they must, love, hold, coddle their babies, but on condition or warding off the danger of any spillages—blood, guts, misery and lust. Their task is to prevent such intensities from going too far, to clean out the drains, on behalf of everyone."

Must we step into the imperial logic of capitalism, by which everything is made to have a price, for women to be compensated for their breastfeeding? Is breast milk a "liquid asset?" The Protestant capitalist model is structured to extract resources for profit and gain rather than to provide reciprocity. More and more, misogyny seems like a tool for society to rid itself of an outstanding, ever-growing debt to women, by devaluing what has been given. Nobody can bear the idea of having been given gift after gift that they cannot reciprocate—or repay. And not only are mothers not paid to breastfeed, but they lose income to do so. Perhaps the golden price tag on breastfeeding and milk might prompt us to re-examine, on a larger scale, why care labor is not properly valued. But I won't hold my breath.

Learning to Loose (2019), from the series *Systems of Attachment*, is a representation of two hanging breasts, one engorged due to mastitis (when the nipple ducts become blocked, causing painful swelling), and the other emptied of its milk and sagging. The breasts fall vertically like a plumb bob, an old construction tool used to measure and determine verticality in a space. The form also recalls the balance tool, an object held by Lady Justice, an allegorical symbol of morality in judicial proceedings, based on the goddess Justitia in Roman mythology. One breast fulfills demand, while the other compensates and suffers in the process. With supply and demand, balance is rarely achieved—resources are depleted and then replenished, tipping the scale over and over again, with little care for the source. One mass

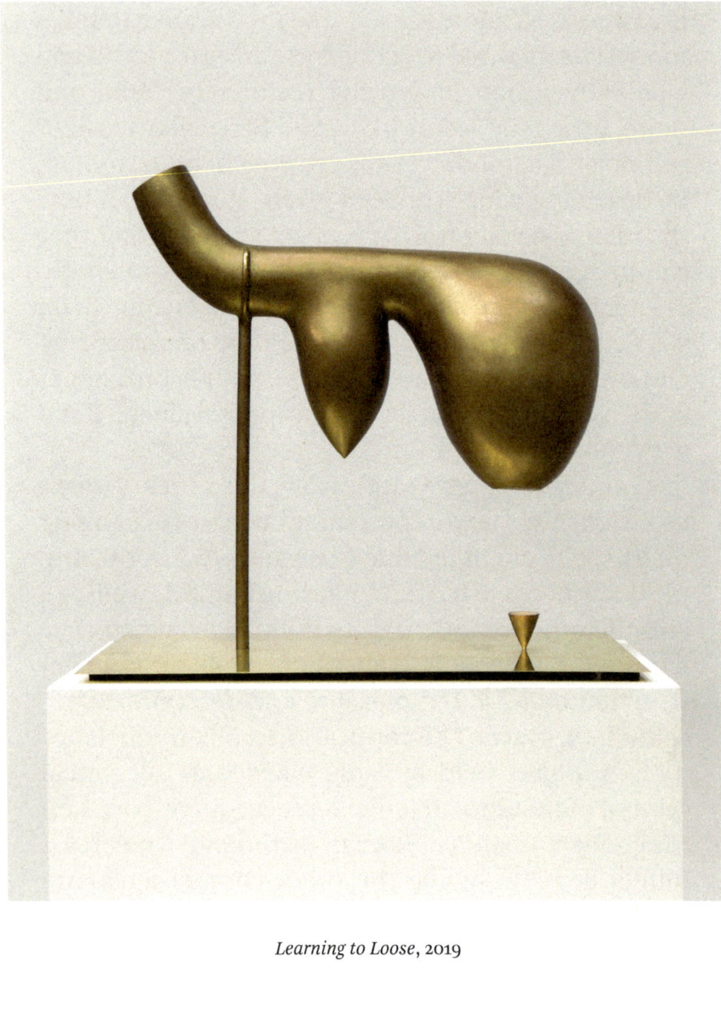

Learning to Loose, 2019

outweighs the other on the scale, and both are ultimately denied their just value.

Once you start pulling the white thread of milk, the whole society's imbalance comes along with it.

1 Paul B. Preciado, *An Apartment on Uranus: Chronicles of the Crossing* (South Pasadena, 2020), p. 62.
2 The now-defunct website www.alternamoms.com, cited by Jacqueline Rose in *Mothers: An Essay on Love and Cruelty* (London, 2018).
3 Rose, 2018 (see note 2).

Sexuality

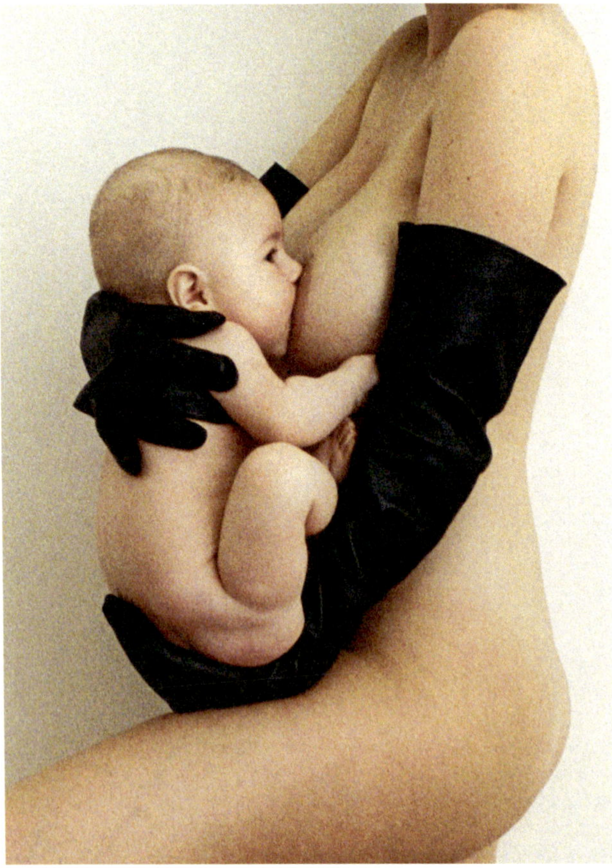

Talia Chetrit, *Feed*, 2020

I am an adult woman and I miss the feeling of my mother's breast. My ideal partner would be my husband, but with breasts. For many people, the sweet, fleshy pleasure of nuzzling your mother's breast never really fades away—my mother touches her own breast when she's feeling insecure, and I've seen other women do the same. I remember coming across a line in a book by Colette where she describes how her family's aide would carry her own breasts like melons when she didn't know what to do. Of course, the pleasure isn't just in touching, but also in being touched—there is a natural link between the maternal and the erotic that begins with the reciprocal, tactile pleasure of breastfeeding. Just look at a milk-drunk baby's eyes rolling back in a state of sensual abandon.

"I have known mothers who stopped breastfeeding simply because they felt they were liking it too much," writes Jacqueline Rose.[1] "The physical pleasure women take in breastfeeding is something rarely talked about. It is the mother's sensuality towards her own children that is the greatest taboo."[2]

I'm wondering if the discomfort some people feel at seeing a mother breastfeed has to do with what they don't see rather than what they do, meaning that everything is covered by the breast. A fully naked body is less erotic than a fragment of a body. A baby sees bodies (its mother's body) not as part of a complete, bigger system that belongs to an individual, but rather as a sort of cartoonish bricolage of disparate elements, like toys in a playground. Each part is graspable and can flee, as if it possessed its own character. In her essay "Visual Pleasure and Narrative Cinema," Laura Mulvey identifies the "pattern of fascination" for the eroticized body as parts rather than a whole. Cinema functions in a patriarchal order, where the woman's body needs to be obliterated from its full reality in order to be desired. Anyone's legs, eyes, nose, mouth, fingers, and toes are suddenly eroticized if you focus on them only. Is eroticism always a return to prelingual fascination? The mother's fragmented body crumbles, stretches, and spreads. It learns how to fall under the weight of gravity in a momentous step. I remember when an older friend of mine feared I would walk in on her in the bathroom and see her naked, and warned, "Don't come in, everything is falling! (*N'entres pas dans la salle de bain, tout tombe!*)"

We are viscerally attracted to the mother, but repulsed by her as well, to avoid an incestual confounding of generations and the terror of a return to the undifferentiated world of fusion.[3] One is reminded of the most famous Greek myth of Oedipus, in which a son inadvertently and tragically marries his mother. The fear of attraction toward the mother is everywhere, structuring how our society functions. The old phallocentric idea that only nubile, childless women are desirable is surely a way to evade reminiscence of the mother's eroticism. And yet, most cases of incest are perpetrated by fathers or father figures on young girls. In contrast to Oedipus, father-daughter relations in Greek mythology give us Adonis, a paragon of masculine beauty—and the transgression is the daughter's fault! Never has myth been so far from reality. The frequency of incest and the overwhelming impunity of perpetrators shows us that it is not only Oedipus who is blind, but society itself. The French psychiatrist Muriel Salmona writes that, in France, one girl out of five, and one boy out of thirteen is a victim of sexual violence. Half of these cases are incest, meaning one girl out of ten. It is said that only thirty percent of sexual abuse cases are even disclosed, so the percentage of the population that has experienced such abuse is even higher.

When I think about incest, the image of Kaa, the snake from Disney's animated-film version of Rudyard Kipling's *The Jungle Book*, always comes to mind, singing "Trust in Me." Because the protagonist, a feral boy called Mowgli, ignores or is oblivious to what he is getting into, he is literally carried, by Kaa, into a situation of subjugation. This appeal to trust pervades all incestuous and incestual relationships (*incestual*, as I understand it, refers to relations that do not necessarily involve sex acts, but rather the miscategorization of the child's place *vis-à-vis* the parent, and vice versa). Contrary to incest, the incestual can be much harder to define, and it is even more deeply woven into Western culture. For example, it is incestual for a father to ask his daughter to dress like a grown woman and to pretend that she is his mistress in a restaurant in order to flatter his ego, as Louise Bourgeois's father did. It is incestual when Serge Gainsbourg plays at incest with his daughter Charlotte as they sing "Lemon Incest."

On the few occasions that maternal eroticism comes into focus, it is difficult not to perceive it as an obfuscation of paternal seduction and aggression, which nobody wants to see, let alone talk about. It is easier to find fault with the mother, because blaming the father means finding oneself at odds with society as a whole. Child abuse is the consequence of patriarchal society, and the silence and shame surrounding it preserve the blindness and tranquility that allow it to continue unabated. It is precisely because sexual violence against children is so monstrously common and so rarely discussed that the sensuality of caring for children has become so taboo, and the sexuality of children so unspeakable in mainstream culture.

Sigmund Freud initially believed that "seduction by the father" and a history of sexual abuse was the cause of "hysteria." He later abandoned his "seduction theory" for a number of reasons, including that "the *father*, not excluding my own, had to be accused of being perverse [...] whereas surely such widespread perversions against children are not very probable."[4] He probably would have changed his mind again if he could have seen current data. The numbers continue to climb following #MeTooIncest in 2021, but the system is clearly not designed to welcome this topic yet, especially in my native France, where victims' speech doesn't even merit basic investigation, where only twenty-five policemen are tasked to the child pornography desk, where France is the third biggest distributor of child pornography, and where the attitudes toward child abuse have consistently been confused with the sexual liberation of the sixties. Recently, both the French right and left have been besmirched by the overmediatized emergence of new scandals, and each side of the political spectrum has used it against the other, but there has been zero progress for victims. In the United States, consider the amplitude of the recent scandal over Balenciaga's advertising campaigns: I would wish that the people who burn thousand-dollar sneakers would invest the same furor into protecting children from the banality of actual physical abuse. Voyeurism into these affairs goes hand in hand with keeping the public in the

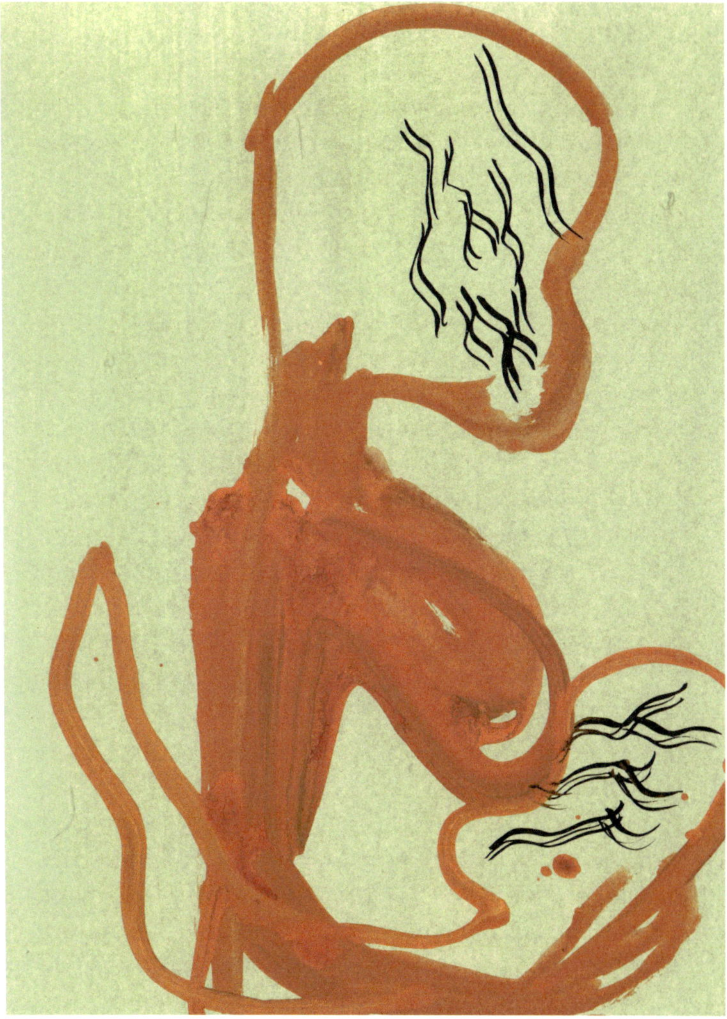

Spoon fed, 2022

dark about how frequently "normal" people (i.e., non-celebrities) perpetrate these crimes against victims who never get to speak about them publicly (or privately).

The willful taboo on children's sexuality maintained by societies in turn undermines a healthy development of our sexualities and their integration into the world, leading instead to anxiety, sexual repression, and the shift from eroticism as a way of being in the world to hedonism as a way of escaping it. In large part, it is in childhood experience that our sexualities are formed: there would be no such thing as kissing if babies didn't suckle at the breast, and being in our mother's womb is the first experience of being "under the sheets." Sex, birth, and childhood are inextricably interwoven, and we should acknowledge that caring for a child is a sensual experience—children's skin is soft, their eyes look like painted enamel, their flesh is perfumed and supple, their bodily care requires tenderness, and the act of breastfeeding is pleasurable. The child's body is tempting, otherwise society wouldn't pretend it isn't. And children themselves want to inspire love.

The explorative sexuality of children, though, is very different from the sexual experience that an adult or an older child might force upon them. For children, such experiences are like living in another language that they do not understand, and thus cannot speak or use to narrate the event. There are many significant reasons why victims of abuse do not report what has happened to them. One is the traumatic amnesia—the brain is oversaturated with emotion and therefore does not "record" the event, a phenomenon described by Salmona.[5] Another is related to how societies react to such stories: victims cannot believe or accept that they are victims. Society describes abusers as monsters, and children understand this literally. "Monsters" exist in fiction—a werewolf, a vampire, an ogre—but a relative, a human being, could not do such a thing to them. The abuser, often a father/cousin/uncle/stepfather/brother, is not a monster, but a family relation, and he can be nice as well, therefore abuse must not have happened. At times the abuse doesn't register as a transgression until years later.

When you have experienced sexual abuse as a child, the nightmare of incest casts a poisonous shadow over your own maternity or paternity, making you fear that you might reproduce the same trauma, or might not be in a position to protect your child from it. I asked Luis Alvarez where parents might draw the line in our everyday gestures. He responded that there is always a sensuality in adult/child relationships, but there are barriers that must be upheld between the genders and generations by the adult, whose role is to set and enforce these boundaries. While it is natural for the child to search for love and attention, including imitating the ways adults look for these things, the parent must never "seduce" the child back. Tenderness without narcissism, love without the expectation of reciprocation. This is the nature of love that children need. No other.

1 Jacqueline Rose, *Mothers: An Essay on Love and Cruelty* (London, 2018), p. 86.
2 Ibid, p. 65.
3 Sigmund Freud, "From the History of an Infantile Neurosis," discussed by Janine Chasseguet-Smirgel in "Being a Mother and Being and Psychoanalyst: Two Impossible Professions," in Donna Bassin, Margaret Honey, and Meryle Mahrer Kaplan (eds.), *Representations of Motherhood*, pp. 113–28.
4 Letter from Sigmund Freud to Wilhelm Fliess, September 21, 1897.
5 Muriel Salmona, "Traumatic Memory: Sexual Abuse and Psychological Trauma," in *Les Cahiers de la Justice*, Vol. 1, Issue 1 (2018), pp. 69–87.

Mother of Tears

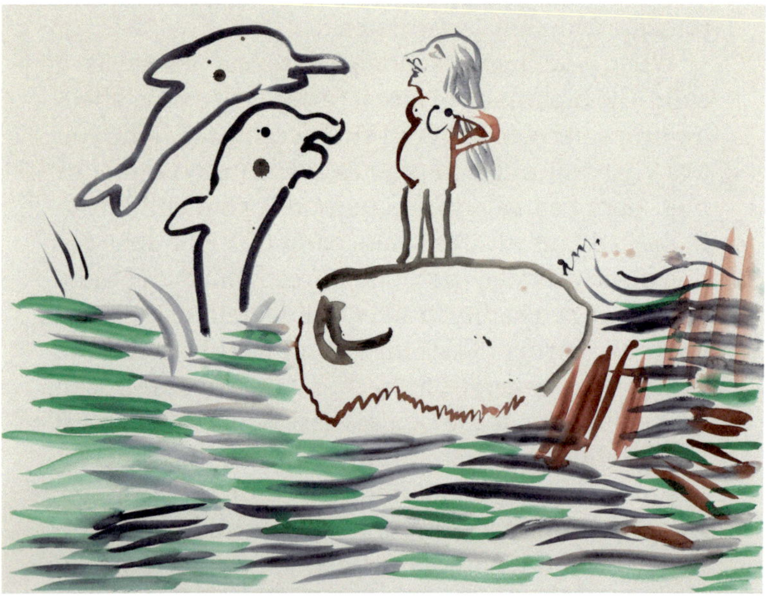

And the Waves Where Have They Been, 2018

> *Pregnancy is a drama [...], one which [the mother] experiences both as enriching and as a mutilation: the foetus is part of her body, and at the same time a parasite exploiting her; she possesses, and is possessed by it; it contains her whole future and, bearing it inside herself, she feels as vast as the world; but this very richness annihilates her, and she feels she is nothing.* – Simone de Beauvoir, *The Second Sex*[1]

My sister's middle name is Alice. When I was a child, the name evoked the surreal adventures Lewis Carroll assigned to her in Wonderland, but I later learned that it had belonged to a family member who committed suicide not long after giving birth.

Early in her journey to Wonderland, in the chapter "The Pool of Tears," Alice grows huge and hits her head on the ceiling. She then begins to cry and floods the hallway with tears before shrinking to the point of having to swim through the deluge of her own making. This push and pull of scale is something every mother experiences: being in the midst of growing physically and psychologically, needing to contend with the impossible idealized qualities of motherhood, while also re-accessing her own childhood and the fears and repressions of that season.

During pregnancy, all of the mother's mental force is channeled toward the child in her womb and the expectations of motherhood, leaving the door to repressed trauma open and unguarded. Past experiences of sexual abuse, incest, negligence, and abandon return in force. As the psychiatrist and psychoanalyst Monique Bydlowski puts it, "During pregnancy, the woman's psyche undergoes a psychic transparency: preconscious and unconscious fantasies and memories of the past are resurfacing. Therefore, the pregnant woman experiences a contiguity with the baby she has been in the past." This direct access to otherwise repressed or occulted memories provides an opportunity for the mother to identify and begin to untie psychic knots that could impinge on her mental health and her relationship with her child. Of course, without adequate support, such as from a psychiatric professional, the cohabitation of too big (child as mother) and too small (mother as child) selves can lead to crisis, depression, and suicide.

One of the most banal causes of postpartum depression is the gap between society's representation of motherhood as a luminous, sugar-coated moment of reciprocal ecstatic family osmosis and the reality of the intense, urgent attention needed by the child and the sheer number of tasks placed on the parent. The cultural and practical baggage of motherhood demands untold renunciation and perseverance, in balanced proportion. It can feel like endlessly circling the drain as energy flows out of you, and the desire to slip down the drain—to disappear into a pool of tears. The lovey-dovey, overly positive discourse on maternity found in advertisements and echoed on social media hide the full-spectrum experience that makes suicide a leading cause of death among women in the first year after their child's birth[2] and the top cause of maternal death in the first three years after a child's birth.[3]

Death lurks everywhere there is life, and especially at life's beginnings. On its own, death is already a great taboo in our society, but it is even more so when in conjunction with maternity and childhood. After

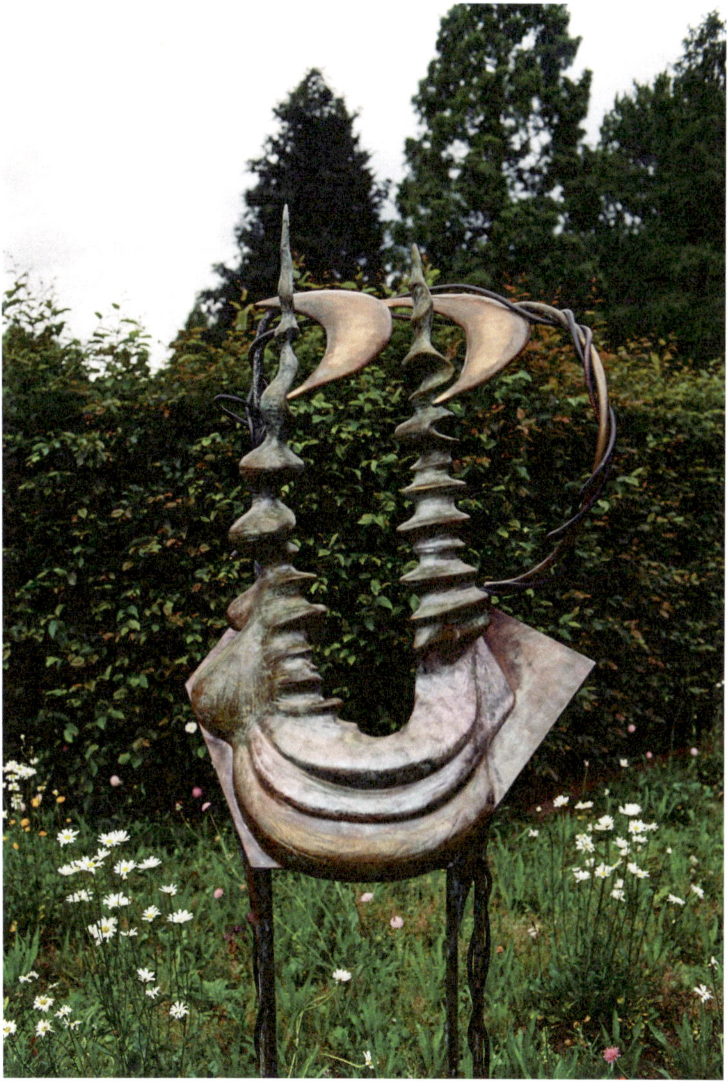

Mon corps de femme, 2019

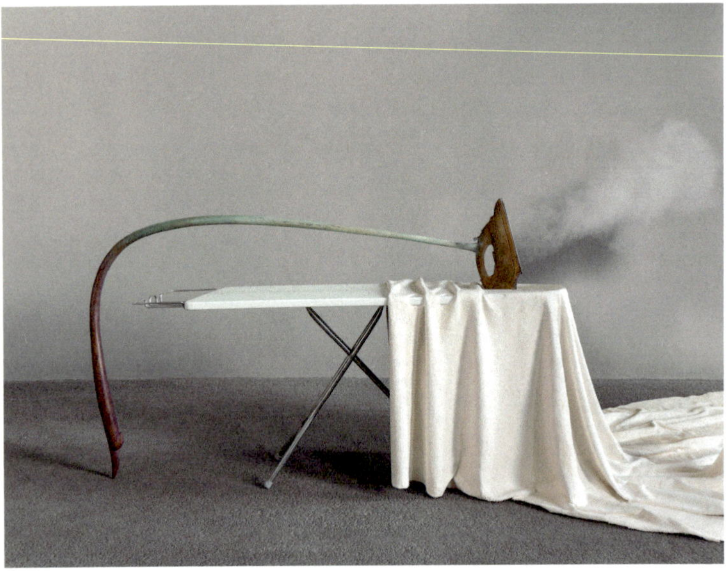

Iron Deficiency, 2021

asking me to guess which hospital department deals with death the most, my OB/GYN in France told me, "It's the maternity ward, but it's the only department without a psychiatric unit that deals with grief." Not long after, I learned that, on average, women have four pregnancies and two children: one abortion, one miscarriage, and two live births. For me, these facts are revelatory and reinforce how necessary it is to have artists and thinkers to help provide spiritual ways of processing and accepting death as part of our lives, and to help open the way toward a framework for accompanying loss in maternity.

I made my sculpture *Iron Deficiency* (2021) with these dynamics in mind. It consists of an ironing table and a body hidden under a sheet, like a ghost with pointy, empty breasts—or a corpse, or a skeleton in the closet. To me, this body, disappeared under a sheet, with its wrinkles of death swiftly hidden and ironed away under a sleek voluptuous and generous veil, is the image of motherhood: the threat of existential death under the disguise of an everyday domestic task. The iron of the title refers variously to an archetypal tool of domestic labor (the clothes iron represented in the piece), to the iron of capitalist industry, to "iron will" that attests to strength and perseverance, and to the greater likelihood of iron deficiency after giving birth. Alice Neel's painting of the *Degenerate Madonna* (1930) was a great inspiration for this work, as were the fatigue, weakness, dissolution, and exhaustion that follow birth and accompany childcare. The vapor that escapes from the clothes iron gestures to the dispersion of the mother's energy, while the pointing finger issues the injunction all mothers are beaten over the head with—you must

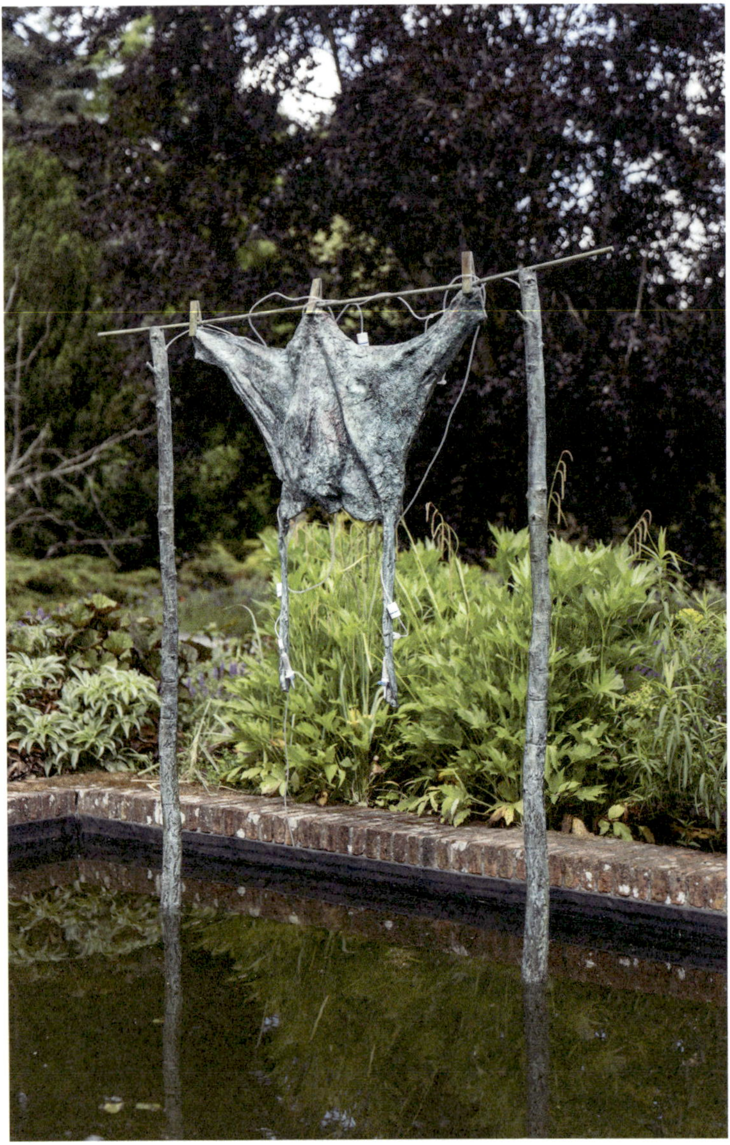

Laundry, 2022

renounce, you must persevere, you must carry on and carry out.

Contemporary society seems to demand mechanical efficiency from us all, not just mothers—but what is conspicuously absent from this regime, what especially stifles and frustrates the maternal in particular, is a refusal to welcome fragility and nuance, to admit death into the presence of life. Each and every person walking down the street has survived gestation, birth, the vulnerability of childhood. We get used to it, but every day preserving our own life and caring for the lives of others around us is a victory that needs to be celebrated.

Will we ever see a public monument to mothers who died in childbirth, to the hospice workers, and others who care for us at the end of life? The only way to access and promote a maternal engagement with the world is to learn to swim through our tears, to learn to tame—and perhaps even to nurture—death, like a stray cat that accepts being stroked and lies down to purr in our laps.

1 Simone de Beauvior, *The Second Sex*, trans. Constance Borde and Sheila Malovany-Chevallier (New York, 1949), pp. 551–52.
2 Amy Tubb, "Maternal suicide still a leading cause of death in first postnatal year," www.maternalmentalhealthalliance.org, December 13, 2019, https://maternalmentalhealthalliance.org/news/maternal-suicide-still-the-leading-cause-of-death-in-first-postnatal-year/ (accessed March 22, 2023).
3 Marie-Claude Mouquet, Sylvie Rey, "Le nouveau suivi de la mortinatalité en France depuis 2012," December 12, 2014, https://drees.solidarites-sante.gouv.fr/publications/etudes-et-resultats/le-nouveau-suivi-de-la-mortinatalite-en-france-depuis-2012 (accessed March 22, 2023).

The Goss

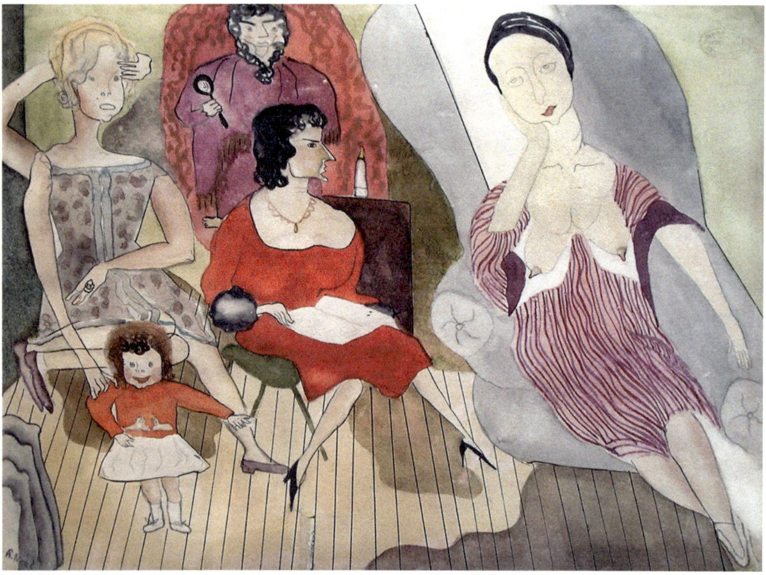

Alice Neel, *The Intellectual*, 1929

In an attempt to write about gossip as an act of resistance, this essay takes the form of a group dialogue—a gossip session in itself. It could be simply read, or also performed as an opera or a play, or with strangers while sitting in the waiting room at the doctor's office. It can also be added to, or gossiped about, ad infinitum by you, the reader, and anyone you choose.

WIKI: The word *gossip* comes from the Old English word *godsibb*, the term for the godparent of one's child. It also referred to people who gathered to help in the birth of a baby, also usually women. In the sixteenth century, the word assumed the meaning of a person, mostly a woman, who delights in idle talk, a newsmonger, a tattler.

MELODY: OK, fine. But what *actually* matters about gossip is the person you're talking about isn't around when you're talking about them.

HARMONY: I think what Wiki is saying isn't that far from what you're talking about. Godparents aren't family, but are inside the family sphere, so this same external/internal dynamic is at work. What the origin of the word gossip tells us is how important words are around children. They can be words to just entertain the mother, but also words to protect herself and the child.

MELODY: Gossip is mumbled *sotto voce* inside, the house about outside the house. But it comes from those kept outside—outside power, outside resources. It's mostly women.

CALLIOPE: And remember, so many of Proust's primary materials came from domestic workers who'd tell him the stories he wove into text.

He'd also turn down invitations to parties so that he could invite people to visit him while he was lying in bed and get the gossip out of people who were there.

ADAM: MAAAMAAAA!

HARMONY: Excuse me, I'll be right back, I've got to go get him.

CALLIOPE: What I was getting at is that gossip is marginalized speech, so it makes sense that it would be associated with women, who are the first outsiders. Its strength comes from a place of helplessness.

WIKI: In *Caliban and the Witch*, Silvia Federici asserts the political and the lifesaving power of gossip for women. Prior to the establishment of justice systems, women's networks were the only resource and means of protecting communities that did not depend on men.

MELODY: Yeah, so like instead of "it takes a village to raise a child," it takes the village's gossip to keep your damn hands off my kid.

CHORUS: The nuclear family killed the village—killed the murmurs that swaddled the children and warned against dangerous men. What we have now is the inchoate internet, each byte a bottle tossed into the sea.

MELODY: Everybody knows it's a question of scale, oh yeah. When it went down, #MeToo felt like this sea change all around the Western world, but its image is waaaay bigger than the reality. In France, the Minister of Justice, the infamous Eric Dupond-Moretti himself, lashed out and said everybody has to watch out for "hysterical women" talking smack. I was so pissed I could've spit nails.

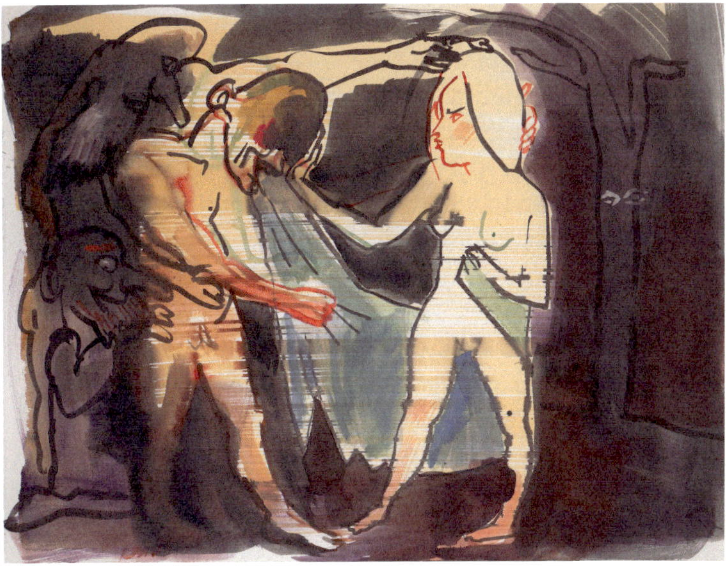

Suzanne and the Old Men, 2019

Of course he didn't use neutral language befitting his station, like "victim's voices" or anything. The blowback is so massive but doesn't get acknowledged, so the whole discussion is skewed and there's this disconnect between the image of the "post #MeToo" world and what is actually fucking happening. I mean, only something like 0.6 percent of rapes get prosecuted!

HARMONY: What did I miss?

CHORUS: We heard through the grapevine that the nuclear family is a nuclear bomb.

HARMONY: Hmm, that tracks ...

CALLIOPE: So like I already said, at its roots, gossip is quintessentially marginalized speech, which is why it's so closely associated with women. But it's not only women's speech. When I brought up Proust, it reminded me that there are definitely passages in *Sodom and Gomorrah* that show how gay people used gossip to identify each other when homosexuality was illegal.

HARMONY: I wonder ... what would you call the kind of gossip used by people in power?

CHORUS: Intelligence?

MELODY: Pretty much anything related to surveillance, really. Tabloids gossip about women's bodies all the time. Politics and finance are packed with whisper campaigns and insider secrets.

HARMONY: So it's the institutionalization of gossip that makes it masculine? That it's in "men's hands?"

CHORUS: Would you pass me the water?

CALLIOPE: I don't know. When it's not institutionalized, it can end up seeming so much more

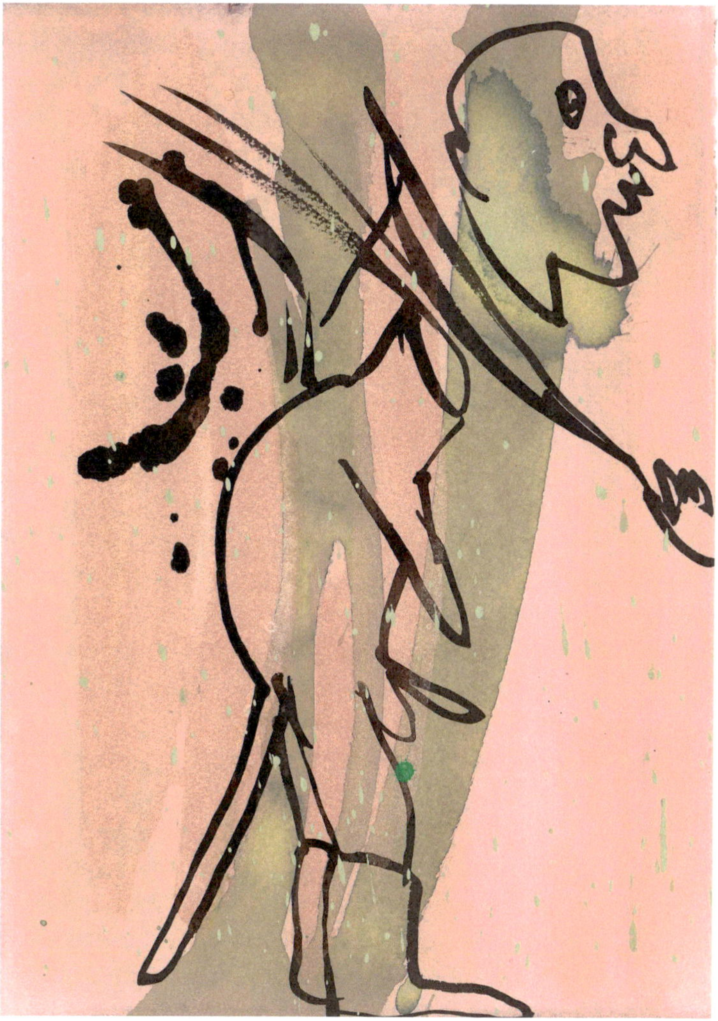

Classée sans suite, 2022

about identity—who's talking about who, and all that.

MELODY: It sounds like you're saying that because gossip is so wrapped up in identity, it shrinks down its meaning and use. Shrink wrap! Harmony was complaining about that the other day. But really, it shows that gossip is all about how, well, the personal is the political.

ADAM: MAAAMAAAA!

WIKI: In *Uncut Funk*, bell hooks and Stuart Hall meet for a series of wide-ranging conversations on what Hall sums up as "life, love, death, sex." Speaking of gossip as "potential pedagogy," hooks describes how, as a child, she would lie down on her aunt's bed and listen to her mother and aunts gossiping, and how those daily conversations would go on to inform her theories and practice.

CALLIOPE: Listening to gossip on a bed is so evocative. There's Proust again, but bedtime stories, too. Like, we're taught that the origin of literature as we know it is epic poetry about warriors, but before anything else, there were bedtime stories and lullabies.

CHORUS: And who do you think was a storyteller and singer?

MELODY: So many of the lullabies I grew up with in France were *dark* if you paid attention to the words or knew the songs' history—they were straight-up stories of domestic violence, murders, sexual harassment, and rape. "C'est la mère Michel," "Jeanneton prend sa faucille," "En passant par la Lorraine," are about sexual harassment, "Au clair de la lune" about forced prostitution, and "La p'tite hirondelle" is about domestic violence … whoa. I only realized it when I started singing Aria to sleep.

HARMONY: Oh, it's not just France. Lullabies sung by enslaved women in the US are full of tenderness mixed with desperation. Gossip and songs connected and consoled people. It gave us the blues, but also gospel.

CHORUS: A gospel chorus isn't all that different from people coming together to gossip. Voices blend together to create rich harmonies. More voices mean more strength.

ADAM: MAAAMAAAA!

HARMONY: Something special can come out of a decentralized group of voices—something a centralized system governed by hierarchy never manages to acknowledge. Like with sexual harassment: any time an institution tries to address it legally, it ends up failing the victims because the first step always involves lawyers and police, with exorbitant costs and misogyny. But with a group, we can protect the harassed. Maybe not officially, but on the ground. As long as we all know what's going on.

MELODY: I don't know anything about centralized/decentralized, but don't you think we need more than an informal justice? Wasn't it Mark Zuckerberg who said, "If you don't want people to know, you shouldn't do it?" But this logic is very Christian—it's assumed that society acts as God, that transparency is a substitute for justice, and that we can deliver a collective judgment. That's not always true.

WIKI: In Dino Buzzati's short story "The Dog Who Saw God," the dog is the gossip. The dog comes to

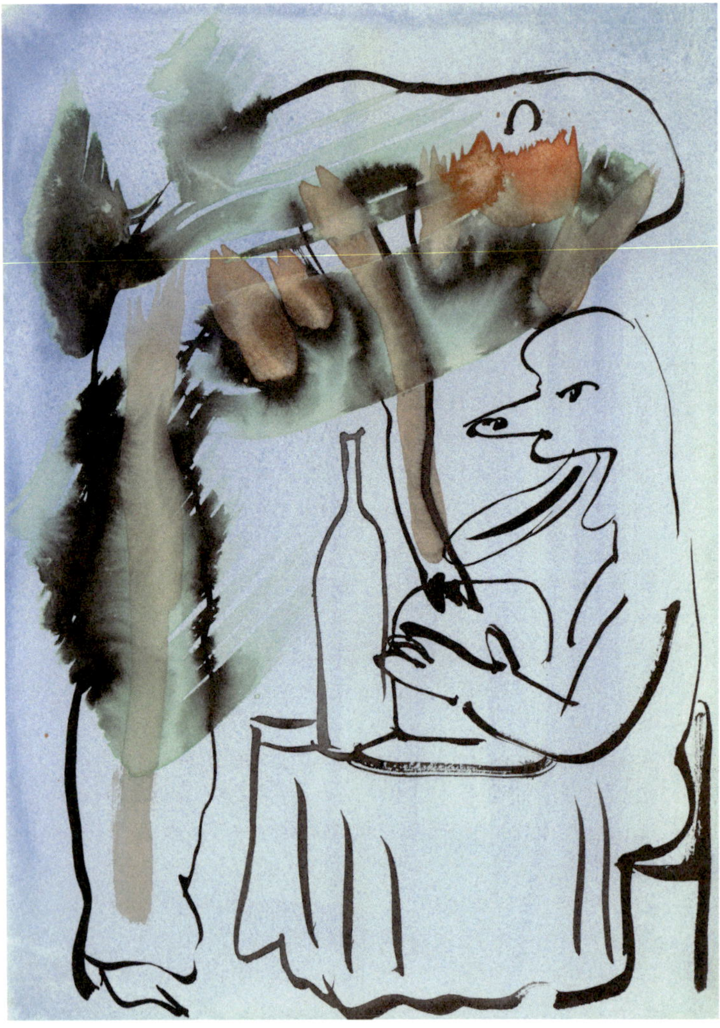

Silently Confused, 2022

sit and watch when something bad is happening. Being watched by the dog is enough trouble that the baker stops beating his wife, and the thief stops stealing bread. For a moment, the village changes its ways. Dog = God. Gossip is killed at the end of the story, and life continues as it was.

HARMONY: Institutions are too slow and murmur is too fast. A bad reputation is a small punishment compared to eternal damnation, or being seen by God. No?

CHORUS: The road is long. Meanwhile, we've got our gossip—our underdogs mostly growl, but when it matters, we can bark, or even howl. Loudly.

Mamas / Mammals

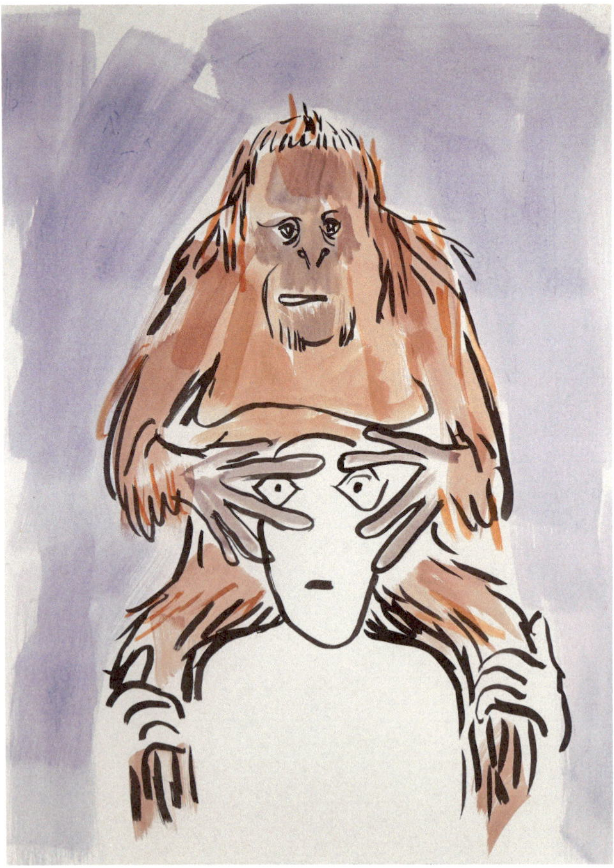

Open Your Eyes, 2020

How do we humans share this cradle, this nest, these surroundings? The plants live together without difficulty. And we? How do we share the air? Without the vegetal world, how do we live together? In fact, it substitutes for the mother.
To Be Two – Luce Irigaray[1]

Not long ago, when I was visiting Liverpool to prepare for the city's biennial, I found myself in the middle of a Fridays for Future protest.[2] I was already in the midst of thinking about a new film project that would try to shape our rational, mediated understanding of the climate crisis into symbols that resonate on the level of the unconscious. I was surrounded by all these young activists with signs like the one reading, "If you don't act like adults, we will," and another that just said, "Seriously!" in childlike handwriting. It made me want to think more about our circumstances in terms of generational conflict and the human life cycle.

My children are too young to make a sign, and I'm too old to skip school in protest. The world I grew up in (the eighties in France) had no WiFi, but there was already an awareness of the danger of pollution. I remember my parents lamenting the pollution of a beach in Brittany we often visited, where we got oil on our skin and in our hair—but it was always talked about from a narrow personal perspective. To this day, I haven't been able to convince them to properly sort their trash.

My generation intuitively understands the climate crisis through the lens of childhood because it presents itself to us as both an image of a past we cannot return to (in which the planet had not yet been pushed to a tipping point) and an image of our future (in our children and their uncertain prospects). For most people born before the turn of the millennium, it is especially difficult to wrap their heads around what's happening because the twin beliefs in an inexhaustible Mother Nature and in boundless Human Invention are so deeply ingrained. Our rational minds know that this isn't the case, but there is an emotional immaturity that positions us as children possessed by outsized power fantasies, and keeps bringing us back to the trope of Earth/nature as an inexhaustible mother, forever fertile and endlessly exploitable.

I recall one ending of my poet friend Jacob Bromberg's maze-poem "Digging for Earth" that reads, "the all-embracing dirt no more a mother than a lover nor a prison than a prism," and how this conception of the maternal Earth can be balanced by an adult relationship to the Earth, with a lover's attentiveness and respect. It is important to identify both as an adult and as a child in the face of climate change. Accepting the loss of the world we knew as children, like the loss of our childhood itself, is a necessary step in order to act and change as individuals and as a society, to become adults in the current ecological context. But unlike a simple and definitive expulsion from Eden, we are required, as responsible adults, to return to a childlike level of learning: to learn the ABCs of zero-waste, the multiplication tables of carbon neutrality, the conjugation of biodiversity protections.

Each child—and each attempt to be as a child—is an opportunity for a new civilizational beginning, a chance to change, to make a radical turn. As anyone who has cared for a toddler knows, the project of civilizing is exhausting but necessary: the fact that a quality is human does not ipso facto make it good. And so part of our task in addressing climate change is to contend with the narcissism of the species. Thankfully, parenthood—and motherhood in particular—provides a built-in way out, insofar as the maternal transcends species. As the philosopher and psychoanalyst Julia Kristeva writes, "If pregnancy is a threshold between nature and culture, motherhood is the bridge between the singular and the ethical."[3]

Throughout the ages, both human and animal mothers have been cast as figures of empathy and care. As opposed to a one-off fix of salvation, these relationships to the other imply sustained attention—what Donna Haraway calls "staying with the trouble." Motherhood is thick with convergences of the animal and the human; the distinction between the two is perhaps shaken most forcefully not by the shared mammalian trait of breastfeeding but by the ability of mammals to breastfeed the young of other species. Romulus and Remus were said to have been nursed by a wolf, Xerxes by a mare, and Zeus himself by Amalthea, often represented as a goat; at the same time, Saint Veronica Giuliani was said to suckle a lamb in her bed, as a symbol of the Lamb of God, physicians once apparently prescribed the suckling of puppies for various medical purposes, and others pass on stories about women breastfeeding monkeys, bears, and deer.

Visiting the zoo with my youngest, Sol, and watching a mother monkey breastfeeding her baby, which had very little hair on its face, I was struck by how similar we were, and realized that despite the compendia of images I've seen, I've never once come across an image of a monkey breastfeeding a human. In the world of images and mythology, things that are too close can not be paired, the same way a dog cannot be a totem animal because it is too close to human society: the actual "parent" of the human race can never be captured in the same family picture. Perhaps it was the guilt of visiting a zoo that prompted this hidden, repressed image to surface.

Our languages are also shot through with these kinds of guilt-laden repressions that wean us from holistic views of nature and our place within it. Language about food in particular creates a cognitive dissonance between animals as subjects with whom we can identify psychically and as physical objects whose meat we ingest: take for instance *pig* vs. *pork*, *cow* vs. *beef*, and so on. Here again, we find mothers at the crossroads—mothers are not just providers of food, but they themselves *are* food for their children.

In 2019, one year after Iddu was born, I started the drawing series *Not Clean Yet*. The series juxtaposes the sense of "getting clean" as meaning something trivial, like potty training, with something as collectively and globally ambitious as reducing carbon emissions. The series interprets this polysemy through the lens of the human life cycle, taking aim at our patriarchal and hypermasculine society's conception of adulthood as the ultimate stage of productivity, which stifles urgent calls for action from the next generation that are more important than prolonging our own comfort and individual growth. By making this cleanliness connection, I wanted

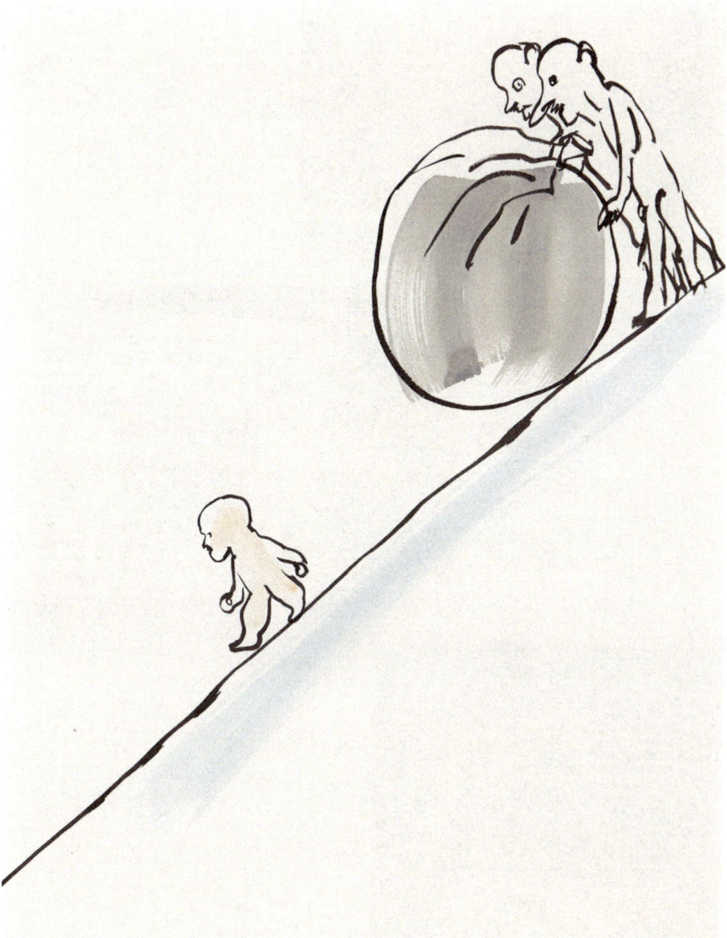

Inheritance, 2020

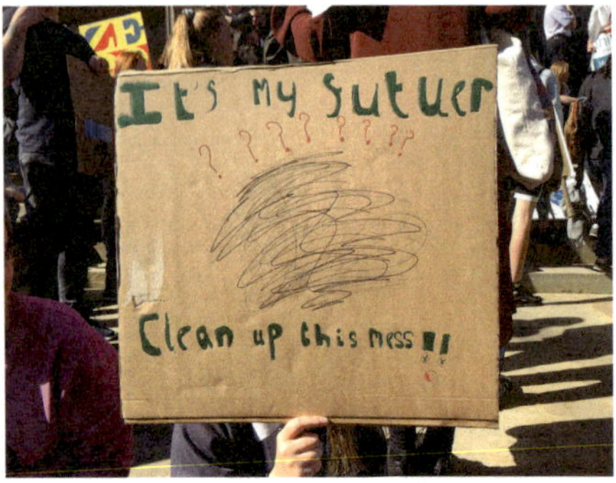

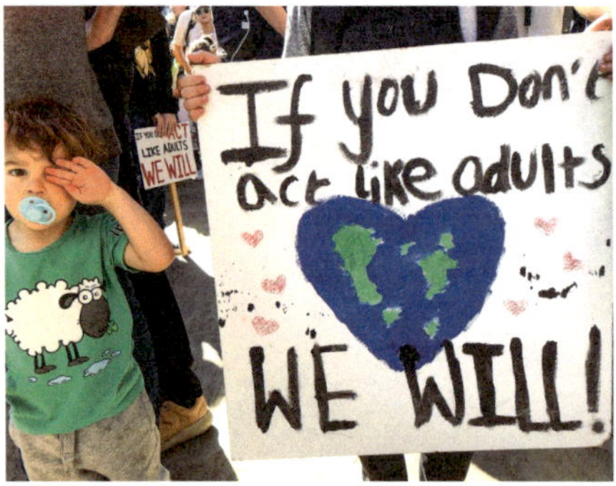

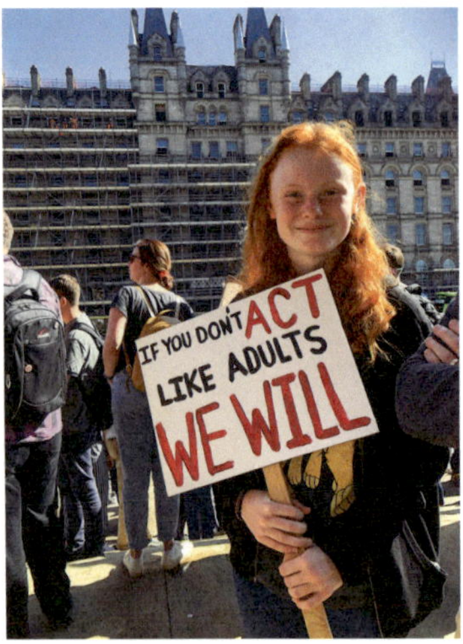

Protest signs at Fridays For Future climate demonstration, Liverpool, 2019

to motivate around climate change from a nuanced position that would show the guilt, the rage, and the imperfections of our actions. As a parent, you are constantly confronted with uncomfortable dilemmas, having to choose between buying your child's horrible plastic dream toy and a biodegradable meeple you'll have to spend an hour coaxing her/him into playing with—between being a good parent and a green citizen. Sometimes it feels so discouraging that it almost seems better to let the world collapse as we look away, since we can never do enough, anyway.

This is the "bourgeois" argument against hope that climate activists face whenever they protest: "Didn't you get here in a car?" "Don't you use a computer?" Ernst Bloch discusses this discouragement in his very relevant multivolume work *The Principle of Hope*, and one can see variations on the same argument everywhere.[4] It's the "down to earth" appeal that people oppose to progressive propositions, which proliferates online, and with particular violence directed at women activists. I wonder if the hyper-scrutinization of women activists has to do with the expectation of women to be "perfect caregivers." The riotous ferocity of the comment sections on an Instagram post by Greta Thunberg or Alexandria Ocasio-Cortez is comparable to the dissatisfaction expressed by a mob of babies to their mother, with the same impossible expectations. The roar on social media is deafening: "If you can't be perfect, be quiet."

The expectation of consistency and perfection is designed to create inertia in precisely the kind of people who want to do things right, who want to take action. Becoming a mother has hammered home the old adage that the perfect is the enemy of the good—it's a necessary mindset to not get discouraged by the amplitude of the task of climate action. Climate action is "crisis management"—nothing "new" is being built.

To properly care requires accepting imperfection, that your tasks are never finished, and that your work will rarely be a spectacle that generates applause. Who still claps for the nurses, domestic workers, and essential workers, who, exhausted by the pandemic, are still doing their jobs? Caregiving requires us to embrace the wild fluctuations of our human commitment and radical changes in our focus and patience. "Care is also a social capacity and activity involving the nurturing of all that is necessary for the welfare and flourishing of life."[5]

We need to accept the glory of maintenance to fully embrace it. For parents and professional caregivers, it is all the gestures of maintenance—feeding, cleaning, and nurturing—that keep a child alive. Day after sleepless night, one diaper after another, size four replaces size three. We learn that things change constantly, and that life is profoundly fragile, especially in its beginnings. We adapt to our children and they to us, and we learn that, yes, we can start again, things can begin anew. If life can be born—and disappear and be born again, through all the miscarried revolutions and obstacles we have borne—all the hopes that life sees grow and die sometimes grow back stronger still.

There are no better words than Hélène Cixous's in her essay "Coming to Writing": "... for the fate of the living I have the untiring love of a mother, that is

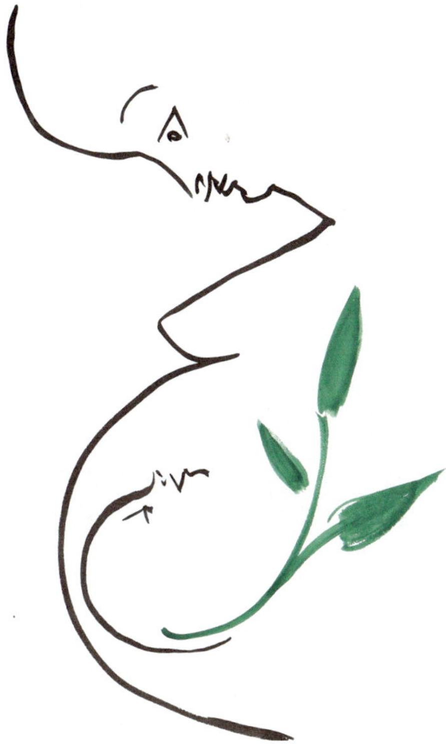

I Need You, 2020

why I am everywhere, my cosmic womb, I work on my worldwide unconscious, I throw death out, it comes back, we begin again, I am pregnant with beginnings."[6]

1 Luce Irigaray, *To Be Two* (New York, 2001), ebook.
2 Fridays for Future is a youth-organized movement that began in August 2018, after fifteen-year-old Greta Thunberg and other young activists sat in front of the Swedish parliament every school day for three weeks, to protest against the lack of action on the climate crisis; https://fridaysforfuture.org/ (accessed March 22, 2023).
3 Julia Kristeva, "A New Type of Intellectual: The Dissident," in Toril Moi (ed.), *The Kristeva Reader* (New York, 1977), p. 297.
4 Written from 1938 to 1947, *Das Prinzip Hoffnung* (*The Principle of Hope*) was originally published in three volumes in 1954, 1955, and 1959.
5 The Care Collective, *The Care Manifesto* (London, 2020), p. 5.
6 Hélène Cixous, "Coming to Writing," in *Coming to Writing and Other Essays* (Cambridge, 1991), p. 48.

Image credits

p. 6 *Untitled (Soon)*, 2019
Ink on paper
88.9 × 118.7 cm
Courtesy of the artist, Mennour (Paris), and Hauser & Wirth

p. 7 *Untitled (Soon)*, 2019
Ink on paper
88.9 × 118.7 cm
Courtesy of the artist, Mennour (Paris), and Hauser & Wirth

p. 8 *Untitled (Soon)*, 2019
Ink on paper
88.9 × 118.7 cm
Courtesy of the artist, Mennour (Paris), and Hauser & Wirth

p. 9 *Untitled (Soon)*, 2019
Ink on paper
88.9 × 118.7 cm
Courtesy of the artist, Mennour (Paris), and Hauser & Wirth

p. 10 Drawing by the artist's son Iddu Linus Henrot Hertig, 2022 (four years old)
Courtesy of the artist

p. 14 Portrait of Camille Henrot, 2018
Courtesy of the artist
Photo: Maria Fonti

p. 18 *Dos and Don'ts – My Bio*, 2021
Digital collage serigraph print with watercolor, ink, acrylic, and oil on prepared canvas
168.7 × 138.5 × 5.9 cm
Courtesy of the artist, Mennour (Paris), and Hauser & Wirth
Private collection, LA
Photo: Marlene Burz

p. 21 *Milkyways*, 2020
Watercolor, acrylic, and oil on canvas
50 × 70 cm
Courtesy of the artist, Mennour (Paris), and Hauser & Wirth
Private collection, China
Photo: Annik Wetter

p. 22 *Dos and Don'ts – True Politeness*, 2022
Digital collage serigraph print with watercolor, ink, acrylic, and oil on prepared canvas
168.7 × 138.5 × 5.9 cm
Courtesy of the artist, Mennour (Paris), and Hauser & Wirth
Photo: Fredrik Nilsen

p. 23 *Dos and Don'ts – Just Believe*, 2022
Digital collage serigraph print with watercolor, ink, acrylic, and oil on prepared canvas
187.6 × 154.6 × 5.8 cm
Courtesy of the artist, Mennour (Paris), and Hauser & Wirth
Photo: Fredrik Nilsen

p. 24 Making of *3, 2, 1…*, Atelier Milome, Romainville, France
Courtesy of the artist
Photo: Charles Milome

p. 27 *3, 2, 1…*, 2021
Bronze, flowstone, polyurethane, aluminum, brass, plaster, steel, wax, wood, various waste materials
325 × 200 × 210 cm (additional waste materials around the pedestal)
Exhibition view, *Wet Job*, Middelheim Museum, June 11–October 16, 2022
Courtesy of the artist, Mennour (Paris), and Hauser & Wirth
Photo: Ans Brys

p. 28 Henrot's mother's taxidermied bird displays, ca. 1988, Paris, France
Courtesy of the artist
Photo: Maud Greder

p. 30 *Untitled (Soon)*, 2019
Ink on paper
88.9 × 118.7 cm
Courtesy of the artist, Mennour (Paris), and Hauser & Wirth

p. 32 *Untitled (Soon)*, 2019
Ink on paper
55.9 × 76.2 cm
Courtesy of the artist, Mennour (Paris), and Hauser & Wirth

p. 35 Mauro Hertig
Excerpt from the score “Mum Hum – Soundscape of an Unborn for 4 performers,” 2021
Courtesy of Mauro Hertig

p. 36 *Every Goodbye* (detail), 2019
Bronze
303 × 80 × 190 cm
Exhibition view, *Wet Job*, Middelheim Museum, June 11–October 16, 2022
Courtesy of the artist, Mennour (Paris), and Hauser & Wirth
Photo: Ans Brys

p. 38 *Words of Mouth*, 2020
Oil on wood
45.7 × 61 cm
Courtesy of the artist

p. 39 Mauro and *Derelitta*, 2016, at Middelheim Museum, 2022
Courtesy of the artist
Photo: Camille Henrot

p. 40 *Inside Job*, 2019, at Art Basel Parcours, 2019
Bronze
265 × 216 × 160 cm
Courtesy of the artist, Mennour (Paris), and Hauser & Wirth
Photo: Franziska Hertig

Iddu and *Every Goodbye* (detail), 2019, at Art Basel Parcours, 2019
Bronze
265 × 216 × 160 cm
Courtesy of the artist, Mennour (Paris), and Hauser & Wirth
Photo: Camille Henrot

p. 42 *The Island / Mothership*, 2018
Watercolor on paper
55.9 × 76.2 cm
Courtesy of the artist, Mennour (Paris), and Hauser & Wirth

p. 44 *Gus Gus DA DA 1*, 2019
Watercolor on paper
55.9 × 76.2 cm
Courtesy of the artist, Mennour (Paris), and Hauser & Wirth

p. 47 *Yours Sincerely*, 2022
Watercolor, ink, and acrylic on canvas
130 × 160 × 4.5 cm
Exhibition view, *Le vers dans le fruit*, Mennour, April 7–May 28, 2022
Courtesy of the artist, Mennour (Paris), and Hauser & Wirth
Private collection, Paris
Photo: Archives Mennour

p. 48 *Un cri du coeur*, 2019
Watercolor on paper
88.9 × 118.7 cm
Courtesy of the artist, Mennour (Paris), and Hauser & Wirth

p. 50 Cartoon by André Hellé in the magazine *La Petite Caricature. Journal de contes joyeux*
André Hellé / Contes Joyeux

p. 53 *Feeling Good II*, 2015
Watercolor on paper
88.9 × 118.7 cm
Courtesy of the artist, Mennour (Paris), and Hauser & Wirth

p. 55 *After School*, 2019
Watercolor on paper
88.9 × 118.7 cm
Courtesy of the artist, Mennour (Paris), and Hauser & Wirth
Private collection

p. 57 Rasmus Myrup
Homo Homo Neanderthalensis (Breastfeeding Daddy), 2020
Pierre noire and sanguine on paper in custom frame
82 × 66 cm
Exhibition view, *Can I Borrow Your Hole*, Last Tango, 2020
Photo: Kilian Bannwart

p. 58 Digital collage with personal photos, model of bronze piece *Learning to Loose*, book *Le Pur et L'impur*, Sony advertisement, and other reference images.
Courtesy of the artist

p. 60 Image from the book *Masters of Erotic Photography*, a Manga cartoon character, Instagram screenshot (@ambera.wellmann) of a painting by Marie Louise Ekman, a screenshot of a sculpture by Liz Larner.
Courtesy of the artist

p. 61 Drawing displaying Alice Neel's painting *Degenerate Madonna* (1930)
Courtesy of the artist and Callie's Berlin
Photo: Olympia Contopidis

p. 62 Printed photo from the artist's binder of reference images for the series *System of Attachment* (2019–21).
Courtesy of the artist

(Clockwise from top left) Printed black-and-white image of Kitagawa Utamaro's print *Pearl Divers* (1802–06), cartoon by Tex Avery, René Girard's *Géométrie du désir*, Instagram screenshots, photo from Lisa Sorigni's series *Behind Glass* (2020), unknown stone sculpture, Wilhelm Reich's book *The Bioelectric Investigation of Sexuality and Anxiety* (1981)
Courtesy of the artist

p. 63 Printed black-and-white detail of Jean Fouquet's *Melun Diptych* (1450), left panel only. From the artist's binder of reference images for the series *System of Attachment* (2019–21)
Courtesy of the artist

Y Woman, 2021, bronze work in production at Atelier Milome, Romainville, France
Courtesy of the artist, Mennour (Paris), and Hauser & Wirth
Photo: Léa Trudel

p. 64 Printed image of Andy Warhol's drawing *Female with Animal at Breast*, ca. 1948–49. From the artist's binder of reference images for the series *System of Attachment* (2019–21)
Courtesy of the artist

Printed black-and-white image of a painting by Hans Schärer *Ohne Titel* (Untitled) (1977)
Courtesy of the artist

p. 65 Instagram screenshot (@olsonstuff) of a man pregnant with an angry child
Courtesy of the artist

p. 66 Printed image of Instagram screenshot (@corydefranco) of Thomas Theodor Heine's illustration *Genevieve* (1911). From the artist's binder of reference images for the series *System of Attachment* (2019–21)
Courtesy of the artist

Personal photo from the artist's binder of reference images for the series *System of Attachment* (2019–21)
Courtesy of the artist

p. 67 Printed image of Instagram screenshot (@williamcult) of a woman and child running from three swans whose upper bodies have the form of Björk in her iconic swan gown. From the artist's binder of reference images for the series *System of Attachment* (2019–21)
Courtesy of the artist

p. 68 Photo of books on desk during residency at Callie's Berlin, 2021
Courtesy of the artist and Callie's Berlin
Photo: Olympia Contopidis

p. 72 *Expressionning*, 2020
Watercolor, acrylic, and oil on canvas
50 × 70 cm
Courtesy of the artist, Mennour (Paris), and Hauser & Wirth
Photo: Annik Wetter

p. 76 *End of Me*, 2021
Bronze, plastic tubing, jeans
230 × 62 × 120 cm
Courtesy of the artist, Mennour (Paris), and Hauser & Wirth
Photo: Annik Wetter

p. 78 *Wet Job*, 2020
Oil, acrylic, and watercolor on canvas
45.7 × 61 × 5.1 cm
Courtesy of the artist, Mennour (Paris), and Hauser & Wirth
Private collection

p. 80 Loie Hollowell
Engorgement, 2021
Soft pastel and graphite on paper
66 × 74.9 cm
Courtesy of Pace Gallery
Photo: Melissa Goodwin

p. 82 *A Free Quote*, 2021
Bronze (hanger), plastic, PU drops
270 × 100 × 40 cm
Exhibition view, *Wet Job*, Middelheim Museum, June 11–October 16, 2022
Courtesy of the artist, Mennour (Paris), and Hauser & Wirth
Photo: Ans Brys

p. 86 *Learning to Loose*, 2019
Bronze
53 × 56 × 32 cm
Courtesy of the artist, Mennour (Paris), and Hauser & Wirth
Photo: Archives Mennour

p. 88 Talia Chetrit
Feed, 2020
Courtesy of Talia Chetrit

p. 93 *Spoon fed*, 2022
Watercolor on paper
38 × 28 cm
Courtesy of the artist, Mennour (Paris), and Hauser & Wirth

p. 96 *And the Waves Where Have They Been*, 2018
Watercolor on paper
55.9 × 76.2 cm
Courtesy of the artist, Mennour (Paris), and Hauser & Wirth

p. 99 *Mon Corps de Femme*, 2019
Casted bronze, electric cables
177 × 66 × 47 cm
Courtesy of the artist, Mennour (Paris), and Hauser & Wirth
Photo: Camille Henrot

p. 100 *Iron Deficiency*, 2021
Bronze (arm, iron), wood board, steel (stand), reinforced acrystal (blanket)
450 × 240 × 150 cm
Courtesy of the artist, Mennour (Paris), and Hauser & Wirth
Photo: Annik Wetter

p. 102 *Laundry*, 2022
Bronze, intravenous tubes, pump
195 × 130 × 30 cm
Exhibition view, *Wet Job*, Middelheim Museum, June 11–October 16, 2022
Courtesy of the artist, Mennour (Paris), and Hauser & Wirth
Photo: Ans Brys

p. 104 Alice Neel
The Intellectual, 1929
Watercolor, ink, and graphite on paper
27.6 × 38.1 cm
© The Estate of Alice Neel
Courtesy of The Estate of Alice Neel and David Zwirner

p. 107 *Suzanne and the Old Men*, 2019
Watercolor on paper
88.1 × 118 cm
Courtesy of the artist, Mennour (Paris), and Hauser & Wirth

p. 109 *Classée sans suite*, 2022
Watercolor on paper
38 × 28 cm
Courtesy of the artist, Mennour (Paris), and Hauser & Wirth

p. 112 *Silently Confused*, 2022
Watercolor on paper
38 × 28 cm
Courtesy of the artist, Mennour (Paris), and Hauser & Wirth

p. 114 *Open Your Eyes*, 2020
Watercolor on paper
88.9 × 118.7 cm
Courtesy of the artist, Mennour (Paris), and Hauser & Wirth

p. 119 *Inheritance*, 2020
Watercolor on paper
55.9 × 76.2 cm
Courtesy of the artist, Mennour (Paris), and Hauser & Wirth

p. 120 Protest signs at Fridays For Future climate demonstration, Liverpool, 2019
Courtesy of the artist
Photo: Camille Henrot

p. 123 *I Need You*, 2020
Watercolor on paper
55.9 × 61 cm
Courtesy of the artist, Mennour (Paris), and Hauser & Wirth

Colophon

Author
Camille Henrot

in collaboration with
Jacob Bromberg, Antje Stahl, and Léa Trudel

Project management
Fabian Reichel

Copyediting
Kimberly Bradley

Graphic design
Neil Holt

Archivist and Image coordinator
Léa Trudel

Typeface
Arnhem

Production
Thomas Lemaître

Reproductions
DLG Graphic, Paris

Printing
Livonia Print, Riga

Paper
Munken Print White Vol. 1.5, 90 g/m²

Published by
Hatje Cantz Verlag GmbH
Mommsenstraße 27
10629 Berlin
www.hatjecantz.com
A Ganske Publishing Group Company

ISBN 978-3-7757-5534-4 (Print)
ISBN 978-3-7757-5535-1 (ePub)
ISBN 978-3-7757-5536-8 (ePDF)

Printed in Latvia

Cover illustration:
Camille Henrot, *where does the words come from?*, 2019.
Courtesy of the artist

With special thanks to Mennour and Hauser & Wirth galleries for their generous support

HAUSER & WIRTH

MENNOUR